COSTA RICA

Paul Glassman

PASSPORT
PRESS

Library of Congress Catalog Card Number 87-63050
ISBN 0-930016-09-2

Photos courtesy of Instituto Costarricense de Turismo

Published and distributed by:
  Passport Press
  Box 1346
  Champlain, New York 12919
  U.S.A.

Printed in the United States of America

Contents

Introduction

In a region where the watchwords are rebellion, repression, corruption and suffering, Costa Rica can be described almost endlessly by what it is not. There is no long tradition of military takeovers. Indeed, there is not even an army, and elections have been free and fair for longer than in many European countries. No class of people has been placed at the margin of society, toiling to enrich a small class of landowners, and the social tensions of neighboring lands are lacking. Typical street scenes reveal few beggars or hustlers, refugees are not the most current export, and almost all people can read and write. Hardly anything happens to attract attention from far away, and no visions of dark, unofficial doings need trouble a traveler to the country.

But for the visitor, Costa Rica is more than a curious island of stability in a strife-torn area. The ordinary historical sites to which visitors elsewhere are taken as a matter of course and obligation are few; but natural wonders and opportunities for sport, adventure and relaxation abound. Volcanoes are at hand for rugged ascent by foot, or in the comfort of a car or bus. Within sixty miles of the capital are cloud forest, dense jungle, sandy beaches, tropical savannah and piney highlands with rushing rivers and white waterfalls. Birds from humdrum sparrow to exotic macaw, beasts from deer to jaguar to monkey, are equally at home. Experienced sportsmen find fishing on two coasts that is unsurpassed in the hemisphere. Comfortable lodging, civilized dining and excellent transportation are all widely available at reasonable prices in a tropical setting that has yet to be heavily traveled. A self-confident people welcomes visitors as equals, not adversaries. There are few surprises but pleasant ones—which is the best surprise.

1

Costa Rica has in the past been covered briefly in guidebooks for all of Central America, and for Costa Rican tourism today, this is too bad. Interest in seeing all of Central America has waned. But facilities in Costa Rica have continued to expand, and curiosity about the country is on the rise.

I hope to help remedy the lack of detailed, current information about travel and living in Costa Rica with this book. History, culture and geography are covered. But this book is also about places and how to visit them; about the capital city of San José and how to live well there at modest expense; about beaches and fishing villages and small towns, and the buses and chugging trains and canal boats that take you to them; about what to take along in your travels and where (and whether) you will find a comfortable place to sleep.

Read this book all the way through if you wish, or consult the table of contents and index to find what you need to know. And if there's something missing, or if you discover in your travels something that you want to share with others, please write to me in care of my publisher.

I hope that you enjoy your visit to Costa Rica.

Costa Rica Large and Small

Costa Rica stretches from sea to sea. Sandy beaches fringed by palms, grassy savannahs, warm inland valleys, temperate plateaus, smoking volcanoes, frosty peaks, forested slopes and steamy jungles succeed each other across the landscape. Twice as many species of trees are native to the many regions of the country as to the continental United States. More than a thousand types of orchids flourish. The national wildlife treasures are still being discovered and inventoried.

Yet, by most standards, Costa Rica is small. From north to south or east to west, the country runs only 200 miles. The shortest distance between oceans is only 75 miles. With an area of 19,575 square miles (50,700 square kilometers), Costa Rica compares to Vermont and New Hampshire combined, or to the province of Nova Scotia. But the influences of two seas and seasonal tropical winds, earthquakes, volcanic eruptions that have enriched the soil, and altitudes that vary from sea level to nearly 4000 meters, make of Costa Rica a continent in miniature.

Costa Rica drapes itself upon a jagged, mountainous spine that runs from northwest to southeast, part of the great intercontinental Sierra Madre-Andes chain. The volcanic Guanacaste, Tilarán and Central ranges, separated from each other by relatively low passes and valleys, rise successively higher down the northern two-thirds of the country. Traversing the south of Costa Rica and continuing into Panama is the Talamanca range, which encompasses the highest points in the country. Cool and even frigid, the mountain slopes remain for the most part in their natural, breathtaking, forested condition, exploited here and there only as pasture.

South of the volcanoes of the Central Range is the Meseta Central, or Valle Central–the Central Plateau, or Central Valley– in every sense the heart of Costa Rica. Measuring only about 20 by 50 miles, the Central Valley covers an area roughly equivalent to that of metropolitan Los Angeles. Yet packed into it are not only the capital city and most of the major population centers, but the richest farmland. Ranging from about 3000 to 5000 feet above sea level, with rolling, forested and farmed terrain, the valley also abounds in natural beauty.

For centuries from the arrival of the Spaniards, virtually the only organized settlement in Costa Rica was in the Central Valley. Even today, this small area is a virtual city-state, dominating every aspect of national life. It claims well over 60 percent of the nation's population, concentrated in the capital, San José, in the nearby cities of Cartago, Heredia and Alajuela, and in dozens of small towns. Almost all industry clusters around the capital. Small farms crowd all cultivable land, producing vegetables for home use, as well as most of the nation's main export crop, coffee.

East of the Central Valley, between the Talamanca Range and the Pacific, is the valley of the General River, which was isolated from the rest of the country until the construction of the Pan American Highway in the 1950s. Here, at elevations lower and warmer than those of the Central Valley, is Costa Rica's fastest-growing concentration of family farms, many operated by migrants from the more crowded core of the country.

Toward the Pacific, Costa Rica tilts precipitously down a slope broken by fast-flowing rivers, some of them harnessed to provide electrical power. In the northwest, on the edge of the hilly Nicoya Peninsula, are miles of sandy beach where Costa Rica's new resort industry is concentrating. Just inland are the savannahs of Guanacaste, populated mostly by fat, grazing cattle. Opposite Nicoya on the mainland is Puntarenas, the nation's major port. Near Panama are some of the more important banana lands, as well as the hilly Osa Peninsula. The remainder of the Pacific coastal area consists of low hills, with a narrow, flat, fertile strip along the water. Temperatures all along the coast are regularly in the eighties and nineties (Fahrenheit), in contrast to the comfortable seventies of the Central

4

Valley.

With its multiple bays, inlets, peninsulas, and hills that plunge into the sea, the Pacific coastline measures more than a thousand kilometers (630 miles), though a straight line from border to border is only half that length. The less broken Caribbean coastline runs only about 212 kilometers (133 miles).

To the northeast of Costa Rica's mountainous spine, the land slopes down to a broad, low-lying triangle of hardwood forest and jungle, with two sides formed by the Caribbean Sea and the 300-kilometer (186-mile) border with Nicaragua. This is the land of eternal rainfall, where coastal storms can blow in at any time of the year. Elsewhere in Costa Rica, the central mountains block Caribbean storms, and it rains only from May to November, when the winds are from the Pacific.

For many years, the eastern lowlands were the impenetrable Costa Rica. Heat, disease, swamps and apparent lack of resources kept the first European explorers even from crossing the area, and the highlands were settled from the Pacific coast. It was only with the construction of a railroad to the sea at the end of the last century, and the immigration of workers from Jamaica, that permanent settlements were established. Even today, communication is difficult and population sparse. No roads disturb the landscape in the forests along the border with Nicaragua, and most transport is by riverboat and canoe.

With its varied climates, the Costa Rican earth can and does produce all the fruits and vegetables of the temperate zones, along with tropical plants, from mangoes, papayas, pineapples and oranges to *chayote, anona, pacaya, zapote* and many others whose names in English are either non-existent or so unfamiliar as to be meaningless.

But for all the diversity of the land, Costa Rica has always relied mostly on a handful of crops. Corn and beans dominated the subsistence scratched from the earth for centuries as a colony, and are still the staples of most Costa Ricans' diet. Coffee, grown in and around the Central Valley, and bananas, grown along both coasts, turned Costa Rica from a poor backwater into one of the better-off nations of Latin America. Sugar, in the lower elevations, and cotton, from the Pacific lowlands, are newer exports, along with beef from the grazing lands of Guanacaste. On these few products, with their rising and fall-

5

ing prices and years of lean and bountiful harvests, the prosperity of the nation depends.

A Short History

Here are some paradoxes:

Hardly a building survives in Costa Rica from the colonial era, though such relics abound elsewhere in Central America. There are few public historical monuments. Yet Costa Ricans, unlike their neighbors, refer almost constantly to the past to explain why they are the way they are; hardly a visitor escapes acquaintance with the country's post-Conquest history.

In museums and shops, exquisite ceramics and wrought gold recall pre-Columbian Indian cultures. Yet virtually no Costa Rican feels a link to the first inhabitants of the land.

The proudest moment in Costa Rica's history was a military intervention in a neighboring country. Yet Costa Rica claims a peaceful tradition of non-interference that sets it apart from other Latin American nations.

PRE-COLUMBIAN COSTA RICA

Even before the first Spaniards arrived, what was to become Costa Rica differed from neighboring lands. To the north, in what are now Mexico, Belize, Guatemala, Honduras and El Salvador, and to the south, in mainland South America, civilizations arose based on the cultivation and harvest of bountiful crops of corn by large groups of settled people. Some societies were so powerful and complex that they altered the landscape with great cities, subjugated peoples for hundreds of miles around, traded regularly with distant lands, wrote histories, and made complex astronomical calculations.

But the Costa Rica of that time was off civilization's beaten track. Armies and traders moved south from Mexico and Guatemala, and north from Peru. Some left their influences in Costa Rica. But none succeeded in dominating the land. Costa Rica was for both cultural regions a distant backwater, removed from the main communications routes. Mountains and swamps impeded passage. Population was sparse. Abundant food and water allowed the native groups to move easily from place to place, which made them difficult targets for conquest. As well, there were few riches in the area to arouse long-term interest by outsiders. Contacts existed between north and south—Peruvian gold and seashells have been found in Mayan tombs—but the path of least resistance was by sea.

The peoples living in Costa Rica when the Spanish arrived belonged to five major cultural groups. Caribs, of South American and Antillean origin, inhabited the Atlantic region. Borucas, related to peoples of Colombia, lived in the lower Pacific coastal area. The Corobicís, the oldest of the native groups, lived in small bands in the valleys of the north. There were also a few Nahuatl-speaking Indians recently arrived from Mexico. The Chorotegas, the most numerous, lived in the Nicoya Peninsula, which was not to become part of Costa Rica until the end of the colonial period. More advanced and settled than the other groups, they cultivated corn and beans for subsistence, and cacao for trade. In all, about 25,000 persons inhabited Costa Rica at the beginning of the sixteenth century, mostly in groups isolated from each other by rivers and mountains and jungles. Even related bands spoke mutually unintelligible languages. They made war on each other, and sacrificed or ate captured enemies.

Archaeologists have been able to trace a shadowy cultural history of the first peoples of Costa Rica, using the objects they left behind. Pottery from Nicoya from before the time of Christ shows similarities to Mesoamerican styles of the period, with red coloring on a buff background. Elsewhere in Costa Rica, pottery was made in a single color, as in South America. A few hundred years later, jade appeared in Nicoya and central Costa Rica, probably imported from Guatemala. The northern influence is evident also in the appearance at the same time of the Mexican god Tlaloc on pottery in Guanacaste, in the northwest. In the sixth century, gold from South America began to appear in southern Costa Rica, possibly following the fall of the empire

8

of Teotihuacán in Mexico, and the disruption of maritime trade routes. By 1000 A.D., multicolored pottery was the norm in Guanacaste and Nicoya, and houses were built in rectangular shapes, all attributes of cultures to the north. Elsewhere in Costa Rica, houses were circular, while pottery featured appliquéd decoration, both characteristics of areas to the south. But while some of the influences of north and south are evident, the dividing line between the two in Costa Rica was generally faint and meandering.

SPANISH OCCUPATION

In densely settled parts of the Americas, the Spanish conquest followed a set pattern. The Spaniards made hesitant contacts with the natives of the coast, learned of a ruling civilization inland, marched to the interior, made war and alliances along the way, and finally subjugated the capital of the native empire, along with everything it ruled. Gold was sought by adventurers, souls by the Church, and glory by both. A new order was imposed, as Indians were parcelled out to Spaniards to be converted, resettled, and put to work. Slaves were imported as necessary to replace those who did not survive war, disease, abuse and outrage. Spaniard married native, and a new set of classes, with the native-born Spaniard clearly on top, replaced in a few decades what had existed before.

In Costa Rica, events took a somewhat different turn, though not for want of effort on the part of the Spaniards. Indian battled Spaniard, but there was no empire to be subdued, and usually no surrender. Riches were elusive, and few slaves were imported. Soldiers and fortune-hunters gave way to subsistence farmers. With the passage of time, the settlement came to have more in common with English and French colonies in North America than with other Spanish dominions.

It was Christopher Columbus himself who discovered Costa Rica, and whose sailors were the first Europeans to be discovered by the natives of Costa Rica. The encounter took place on or soon after September 18, 1502, when Columbus, on his fourth voyage to the New World, took shelter from a storm at what is now Uvita Island, just off the port of Limón. No account survives of the impression that the intruders, with their white skins and huge ships, made upon the natives. But the Spaniards noted straight off the golden disks and animal-form decorations worn by the inhabitants, and acquired some of them in exchange for junk jewelry. And through native playfulness or cunning, or faulty interpretation, or wishful thinking on the part of the newcomers, the Spaniards departed with the impression that there were treasures aplenty in all landward directions. Thus, and with similar exchanges on succeeding expeditions, did the nickname of Costa Rica—the Rich Coast—become applied to the land that the Spaniards officially called Veragua.

Attempts to subdue the land and its peoples, and appropriate its reputed treasures, however, faltered. A party led by Diego de Nicuesa in 1506 explored the Atlantic coast of present-day Costa Rica and Panama. But the close-knit native bands viewed all outsiders with mistrust, and none made the fatal mistake, so common elsewhere, of allying itself with the newcomers against traditional enemies. Attacked by Indians who vanished into the jungle, ravaged by heat, diarrhea, yellow fever and assorted diseases to which they had no resistance, tormented by clouds of mosquitoes, drenched by seemingly inexhaustible rains, bogged down in mud, unable to replenish supplies, the men of the Nicuesa party departed without founding a permanent settlement, and later expeditions likewise came to grief.

Frustrated on the Atlantic side, the Spaniards turned their efforts to the Pacific shore. Here the terrain was less of a morass, the vegetation less impenetrable, the inhabitants more permanently settled and less intractable. Spanish attempts to conquer were less of a failure. The expedition of Gil González Dávila in 1522 succeeded in peacefully converting many Chorotega Indians under Chief Nicoya to Catholicism. Quantities of gold were carried off as well. The price was over a thousand men dead from the familiar trio of hunger, disease and raids. Francisco Fernández de Córdova later founded a town called Bruselas near present-day Puntarenas, but infighting among Spaniards led to its abandonment. Short-lived settlements were established on both coasts, but for more than half a century from the arrival of Columbus, there was no permanent Spanish foothold. Finally, in 1561, Juan de Cavallón, with a party of Spaniards and domestic animals, founded the successful settlement of Garcimuñoz in the Pacific lowlands. For lack of finding gold, however, Cavallón himself withdrew.

It was under Juan Vásquez de Coronado, Cavallón's successor as governor, that Costa Rica's course began to differ from that of the other Spanish provinces. Vásquez moved the main settlement from the lowlands to the temperate Central Valley, and renamed it Cartago, or Carthage. The search for gold was abandoned, and Vásquez attempted to deal with the natives in friendship. Spaniards cultivated crops for their own consumption, lived mostly in peace, but achieved no great prosperity. Cartago was not the sort of outpost that attracted adventurers, but at least it survived. The luck of Costa Rica in being governed by Vásquez, however, did not extend to him personally: he was lost at sea after a voyage to Spain to seek financial aid for the colony.

COLONY AND NATION

Despite the initial peaceful settlement of the valley, conflict with the natives was inevitable, and the Spaniards dealt with them in characteristically harsh fashion. A few were subjected, and came to live peacefully alongside the Spaniards, to serve them and eventually to intermarry with them. Others were conquered and removed to areas where they could be easily watched over. By far the largest numbers refused to submit. Some simply moved on to remote areas of the lightly populated country. Most either died violently or succumbed to the diseases brought by the Spaniards, to which they had no resistance. There was no Indian problem in the parts of Costa Rica settled by Spaniards simply because there were soon few Indians.

Without native labor to exploit, without crops to grow for export on a large scale, restricted in trade by Spanish mercantile policy, hemmed into a small valley by hostile environments, Costa Rica stagnated, and the very name of the colony must at times have seemed a cruel hoax. No great public buildings were erected. Little moved out of the province but small amounts of meat, cacao, honey and potatoes. Traders faced a journey to port made hazardous by Indians. Sea traffic was ravaged by pirates. Manufactured goods were in short supply. Costa Rica was virtually isolated from Nicaragua, and communication with

Panama existed only by a mule trail that was often impassable.

Spain responded to piracy by closing the ports in 1665. Trade plummeted, though smuggling to Panama and illegal contacts with Dutch and English merchants continued. The shortage of money forced the colonists to revert to the traditional Indian medium of exchange, cacao beans. Cloth was so scarce that tree bark and goat hair were used to make clothing. Even the governor had to grow his own food.

The forlorn colonists remained isolated on their farms, not even coming to town to attend church, not least because they had nothing to wear. Family life was disorganized, and church officials complained of the licentiousness of the populace. A few immigrants drifted in, but the colony hardly grew; more than a hundred years after its founding, Cartago, the capital, was barely more than a village, with fewer than a hundred houses, and a single church. It was destroyed almost entirely by the eruption of the volcano Irazú in 1723.

Costa Rica's last century as a colony saw some improvement in the standard of living, and even a modicum of prosperity. Religious authorities, alarmed at the depths of poverty and ignorance, the low level of morality, and their declining influence, in the late eighteenth century ordered the populace to resettle and concentrate around the churches. Trade with the other colonies was officially re-opened toward the beginning of the eighteenth century. Cacao plantations near the Caribbean expanded as the coastal area was fortified, and by the end of the eighteenth century, Costa Rica was exporting tobacco, sugar, wheat and flour, as well as cacao. To the first towns of Cartago and Aranjuez were added Heredia, San José, Alajuela and Escazú, all organized in the eighteenth century as agriculture and settlement pushed westward from Cartago.

But progress was relative. In comparison with its neighboring colonies, Costa Rica remained poor, isolated, sparsely populated, a social misfit in its lack of a class structure. There were probably no more than 20,000 persons in Costa Rica at the opening of the nineteenth century, most descended from the few score families that had first settled the colony. Less than one-eightieth of the land had any significant settlement.

Independence, when it came, had little initial effect on Costa

Rica. Spain had administered the five Central American provinces from Guatemala; toward the end of the colonial period, Costa Rica was reduced to the status of a dependency of Nicaragua. In practice, however, Costa Rica had long gone its own way. Without the ambitions and class conflicts of the other colonies, living at subsistence, Costa Rica required only minimal government.

News of the independence of Central America, declared in Guatemala on September 15, 1821, reached Costa Rica at the end of the year. A provincial government was hastily formed, and soon acceded to annexation to Mexico. Opinion on the association was divided, however, and a short civil war was fought. The forces of the town of San José, rejecting Mexico, gained the upper hand. In the end, the Mexican empire collapsed in 1823, and Costa Rica joined the United Provinces of Central America, with full autonomy in its internal affairs. The most important result of independence was the elimination of Spanish trading restrictions, but since the world was not beating a path to Costa Rica's door, even this freedom was of limited value.

With little administrative heritage from Spain, Costa Rica's form of government varied over the years. At times it was frankly experimental, as legislatures changed from bicameral to unicameral and back again, and the capital was rotated between towns on a trial basis. Internal strife also came with independence, though to a lesser degree than elsewhere in the region.

Costa Rica's first elected president, Juan Mora Fernández, held office until 1833, and began the policy of encouraging coffee cultivation. Civil war broke out toward the end of his term over the location of the capital. Braulio Carrillo, chosen for the presidency by congress in 1835, succeeded in stabilizing the country politically and financially, and planted the capital firmly in San José. Carrillo extended his term by coup d'etat, and ruled as a benevolent dictator until overthrown in 1842 by Francisco Morazán, a Honduran and Central American federalist. Morazán's extra-national ambitions led to his own overthrow and execution in 1843.

Costa Rica made do with a weak central government after Morazán, and even abolished its army for a short time. In 1848, all connections with the long-moribund Central American federation were severed. A strong leader emerged once again in 1849

13

with the election to the presidency of Juan Rafael Mora, a representative of the new coffee aristocracy.

Mora's term saw the one glorious military episode in Costa Rica's history. The American adventurer William Walker had taken control of Nicaragua, and Mora responded to the challenge by raising an army to oppose him. Aided by Britain and by American business interests, Costa Rica played the major role in ousting Walker from the isthmus.

Following the Nicaraguan adventure, Mora was overthrown, and was subsequently executed when he attempted a comeback. A military government gave way to a series of constitutional presidents who represented the aristocracy. In 1879, Tomás Guardia overthrew the government, and ruled as a military strongman until his death in 1882. The presidency then passed in turn to two of Guardia's relatives.

DEVELOPMENT AND EXPANSION

The topsy-turvy politics of Costa Rica in the nineteenth century were only a sideshow to the economic changes that were taking place. Costa Rica was transformed, as coffee came to be cultivated on a large scale.

Coffee was first grown in Costa Rica toward the end of the colonial period. The plant was so eminently suited to the highland volcanic soil and held such obvious promise that the newly independent republic granted it exemption from a number of taxes. By 1829, coffee was Costa Rica's most important product. In 1831, the government began to give away land on which to plant the crop. Production grew from 50,000 pounds in 1832 to 9 million pounds in 1841, and by the 1880s, annual harvests approached 100 million pounds.

Inevitably, the rewards of coffee cultivation were not distributed evenly. Some families acquired large expanses of land, transformed their wealth into political power, and developed tastes for culture and the finer things in life that the nation had done without for so long. But despite the emergence of a class structure, there appeared to be land and profit enough for all, and no sector of society failed to advance.

Although he was autocratic, Tomás Guardia saw himself as a

benefactor of his people. Under his government and those of his two successors, roads were built and improved, public buildings erected, capital punishment abolished, and primary education made free and compulsory and independent of the church. Coffee earnings, and borrowings against future earnings, financed the expenditures.

The problems of shipping coffee led indirectly to the development of a second major export crop. Coffee was sent by oxcart to the Pacific port of Puntarenas, then on a long voyage around South America to markets in the eastern United States and Europe. To shorten the journey, President Guardia ordered the construction of a railroad line to the Atlantic. Bananas were planted as a stop-gap measure to provide revenue for the financially troubled project. The new crop proved immensely profitable, and large areas were soon planted in the fruit.

DEMOCRATIC COSTA RICA

Costa Rica's modern, democratic tradition started with the election of 1889, the first that was honest, open and direct. No masses clamored for reform at the time. In a typically Costa Rican way, President Bernardo Soto called for the free election whose time, he felt, had come. José Joaquín Rodríguez, a candidate opposed by Soto, won the election and, against expectations, took office. The course of democracy was to have its ups and downs thereafter. Presidents attempted to amend the constitution in order to succeed themselves, and dismissed uncooperative legislatures. But peaceful transitions of power, and more active participation in politics by all sectors of the population, characterized the years that followed.

The major challenge to the democratic trend came in 1917. Claiming that the government was corrupt, Minister of War Federico Tinoco Granados seized power and ruled as a dictator. Opposition by the United States helped force his resignation after two years, and elections were held for a successor.

In the 1930s, Costa Rica began to show signs of social unrest. Many of the benefits of coffee wealth had gone to relatively few families. An extraordinarily high rate of population growth had led to repeated division of the smaller landholdings, and many

15

workers owned no land at all. A strike in the banana plantations succeeded in obtaining higher pay, and agitation was threatened elsewhere.

The response of those in power was to take the lead in distributing wealth more evenly and improving the security of workers. President Ricardo Jiménez Oreamuno organized a government insurance company, and in 1935 began the distribution of United Fruit Company land to farmers, in small plots. Under Rafael Angel Calderón Guardia, a physician who became president in 1940, the measured pace of reform continued as the first social security legislation was enacted.

Calderón was to be one of the more controversial figures in modern Costa Rica. His social programs—including paid vacations, unemployment compensation and an income tax—and his early declaration of war on Germany, offended many of his original conservative supporters. Calderón sought to broaden his political base by allying himself with the Communist-influenced Popular Vanguard party. The polarization of the country continued under Calderón's successor, Teodoro Picado. Conservatives considered the government radical, while liberals, led by José Figueres Ferrer, felt reform programs were ineffective.

In 1948, Calderón ran again for the presidency, and lost to Otilio Ulate. But the government claimed fraud, and the legislature annulled the results. Tensions rose, and finally broke out into an open rebellion led by José Figueres. Armed by the governments of Guatemala and Cuba, the rebels prevailed in a few weeks over the army. The short civil war was the bloodiest in Costa Rica's history, with more than 2000 killed.

MODERN COSTA RICA

José Figueres led an interim administration that attempted to restore order to a disrupted nation. Banks were nationalized and taxes restructured. Most curiously following a civil war, and amid threats from domestic plotters and opponents in exile, Figueres and his allies chose not to purge and restructure the army, but to abolish it altogether, retaining only those elements of the old security forces that they considered appropriate in the Costa Rican context: a national police force, and the mili-

16

tary bands.

A constituent assembly proceeded to write a constitution that rejected some of Figueres' proposals, but extended social welfare programs, gave the vote to women, ended discrimination against blacks, and established an electoral tribunal with broad powers to ensure the honesty of elections. Following the legislative elections of 1949, Figueres stepped aside, and Otilio Ulate, the victor of the disputed 1948 vote, assumed office as president.

Despite the bitterness of the civil war, politics in Costa Rica since 1948 have been remarkably peaceful and democratic. Exiles have threatened invasions on two occasions, but have found no internal support, and their movements have fizzled. José Figueres himself has twice served as president, from 1953 to 1957 and from 1970 to 1974, and his National Liberation Party has dominated electoral politics. But it has only once held the presidency for more than a single term.

Social and economic progress since 1948 has contributed to stability. With revenues growing as a result of high coffee prices, the government has acted to improve living conditions and modernize agriculture and industry. By 1981, social security programs—medical care, health services and income maintenance —served 90 percent of the population, took 40 percent of the national budget, and were the largest employer in Costa Rica. Education accounted for 30 percent of the budget, and basic schooling was widespread. Government clinics and private agencies have provided birth-control information to a people concerned not with surviving but with maintaining its standard of living. A population growth rate that was one of the highest in the world at mid-century was reduced from over four percent to well under three percent. Life expectancy has meanwhile risen to 68 years for men and 72 years for women, respectable figures for any country.

Economically, Costa Rica has diversified considerably. Industry expanded at phenomenal annual rates of over ten percent in the sixties, as manufactured goods were exported to the new Central American Common Market. Exports to other areas remained largely agricultural, but expanded to include meat, lumber, sugar, cacao and flower seeds, along with coffee and bananas.

17

Massive public works have helped to improve living standards. Hydroelectric projects have brought power to most homes in the Central Valley. An intracoastal canal along the Atlantic has improved access to parts of the lowlands. The highway system has been extended even to the once forbidding Caribbean region. Government land continues to be available to those who are willing to work it. Foreigners and foreign investment have been equally welcome, and tourism has grown, as have the numbers of retired residents from abroad.

But not everything has been rosy for Costa Rica. Unstable coffee prices, oil bills, disruptions of trade in the Central American Common Market, and the costs of social programs have all given the society and economy a jolt in recent years. The government has at times been hard-pressed to meet payments on loans from abroad, and the currency has been regularly devalued. National income has fallen in some years, and unemployment has risen.

Elsewhere in the region, economic crises of these proportions have led to turmoil and bloodshed. In Costa Rica, administrations that have failed to stabilize the economy have been turned out of office democratically. But while Costa Ricans are proud of their stability, it has provided little consolation when they have had to make do with less.

Internationally, Costa Rican foreign policy has varied from president to president, while remaining generally pro-Western. Most recently, Costa Rica has actively sought reconciliation between all parties in conflict in Central America. For his key role in putting together a peace plan, president Oscar Arias was awarded the 1987 Nobel Peace Prize.

A Mystery of National Character

"The Switzerland of Central America"... "more teachers than policemen"... "peaceful and idealistic"... "no sharp class distinctions"... Costa Rica sometimes sounds like an earthly version of heaven, where all live in peace, and the cares of a less civilized age have been transcended.

No nation could live up to such a billing, however, and the facts bear sorting out. The relative lack of beggars and street urchins indicates that in at least *this* Central American country, there is a minimal social justice. Citizens do, indeed, respect authority and national institutions, rather than fear them.

But there are also elements of more fallible societies. Most Costa Ricans are moderately poor, though poverty is buffered by social services. The bloodiest war in the nation's history occurred only 40 years ago, political exiles have attempted, unsuccessfully, to invade and stir general uprising, and terrorist incidents, attributed to foreigners, have occasionally taken place. There is no army, but the police forces are organized along military lines. As in other parts of Latin America (and in many "advanced" countries), though to a much lesser degree, corruption is part of the way things work.

Still, in its usual state of social peace, in its profession of and adherence to democratic values, Costa Rica is more like nations in North America or Europe than its seething neighbors. It is the social democracy, rather than the Switzerland, of Latin America. That it is so is the primary mystery of the place to many first-time visitors.

There are no easy explanations, no easy descriptions of this regional anomaly. Costa Ricans are Latins, like most of their neighbors to the north and south. But they are a paler shade of

Latin. Literally this is so, for though Costa Ricans come in all colors and mixtures of European, native American and African, the European strain predominates. But also in their ways, Costa Ricans are just like their neighbors, only—to turn an ethnic punch-line around—less so. Costa Ricans profess the sanctity of the family as much as other Latins, and social life centers on the home, but the family is not quite the unassailable bastion of elsewhere. Catholicism is ingrained in national life, but public displays of religious fervor are relatively restrained. A Costa Rican male will maintain as strongly as any Latin that sex is a major occupation or preoccupation, but unbridled machismo is rare.

Why are the Costa Ricans a little bit different? Relative prosperity, inevitably, has something to do with it. But a few American nations have had fortune and circumstances comparable to those of Costa Rica. Argentina comes to mind immediately as a country that is fairly well off, even more European-descended than Costa Rica, and mostly middle class. Yet Argentines as a whole are volatile and ultranationalistic, and so fractious in their political expression that many consider dictatorship a necessity to sort themselves out. Costa Ricans are nothing of the sort.

Costa Ricans themselves usually find the explanation in their history. The national myth that informs the way Costa Rica looks at itself arises out of the hardships of the colonial period. In that time, all were small farmers, equally poor and equally proud; all had to labor to sustain themselves. There were no slaves, no social classes, no wealth for anyone to accumulate, nor differences of race or privilege. No man could hold himself to be the better of another. Colonial Costa Rica was a natural democracy.

The national myth is, indeed, only a myth today. Costa Ricans are no longer equally poor. Opportunities to advance did finally present themselves in the era of coffee expansion, and there were no barriers to getting ahead other than those of talent and will. Most Costa Ricans now aspire to be part of the middle class, and a few are wealthy. But they still uphold equality of opportunity, independence, self-reliance and hard work, converted from everyday facts of colonial life into generally accepted values. The heritage of social tensions of other Latin American

20

countries—race against race, class against class—is not ingrained, if not entirely missing. Individually and as a nation, Costa Ricans erect fewer barriers against each other, and against outsiders.

Not everything about the Costa Rican character, however, is unique, different, or even positive. Some of the shadings of variation from neighboring lands are rather delicate, and easily over-emphasized. Nobody who visits Costa Rica has any doubts about what region of the world he is in. Attitudes about time are relaxed, bureaucracy is stifling, and logic sometimes follows a non-western course. But few fail to notice, as well, a fresh air of difference.

To themselves, and to those who know them, Costa Ricans are *Ticos*. The nickname derives from the way they speak. Diminutives are common in the language of Latin America. A moment becomes a "little moment," a *momentito*, to indicate "in a little while." But in Costa Rica, the word is *momentico*, and the peculiar ending is applied to the people who use it.

Like their Spanish language, which was locked away for centuries from the outside world by mountains, jungles and seas, Costa Ricans are gracious, courteous, traditional, even a bit archaic. The *retrete*—that circling of boys and girls in the central square on weekend evenings, with shy glances that could, just could, lead to romance—hung on in Costa Rica even as it was disappearing from elsewhere in Latin America and Spain. Now, dating has replaced the custom. But old-fashioned prudishness survives. Movies, for one, are heavily censored.

The sense of tradition and what is proper extends to marriage, of course. Most couples are married in church, and the common-law unions that elsewhere in Latin America may outnumber legal marriages are in Costa Rica the small minority. Marriage is usually life-long. Divorce is technically legal, but scandalous. If a marriage fails, the family stays together, though a husband sometimes spends his nights away from home. And even in successful marriages, the sexual wanderings of men are said to be tolerated, while women's are limited by social pressures and home duties; though how this may be is, of course, a great statistical mystery.

More than 95 percent of Costa Ricans are Catholic. The government contributes money to the Church, and religious education is part of the public-school curriculum, though technically optional. The missionary Protestant evangelism that has spread to Latin America from the United States has so far had little impact in Costa Rica. Sudden modernization, disruption of isolated village life, prolonged warfare, natural disasters, and the hopeless poverty that elsewhere have loosened ties with the traditional church exist to a lesser degree or not at all in Costa Rica. Some Protestant sects have their headquarters in San José not because Costa Rica is a fertile field, but because it is centrally located for their Caribbean and Central American efforts, and because life in San José is pleasant.

Catholicism is so unchallenged in Costa Rica that it is somewhat taken for granted. Men especially are lax in their practice, and for many persons, baptisms, weddings and funerals are the only occasions for seeing the inside of a church. Religious holidays dot the calendar, and the saints' days of the towns and villages are regularly celebrated. But mystical devotion that transcends the hardships of everyday life is simply not part of the Costa Rican national experience. Fiesta processions pale before those of other Latin American countries. The country is short of priests, and most of the clergy is Spanish, Italian, Irish or American, rather than Costa Rican. Nevertheless, if challenged, as they sometimes are by missionaries, Costa Ricans will feel their allegiance to the Church becoming stronger.

Civic pride is said to be the second great religion of many Costa Ricans. The *fiestas cívicas*—the year-end celebrations—bring out more parades, floats, dancing, puppeteers and music than any church commemoration. And national elections—when the peaceful governmental tradition is most evident—are the occasion for the largest celebrations. Costa Ricans are conscious that their national traditions and values differ from those of their neighbors, and are protective of their separateness. To outsiders, they may be Latin Americans. And a Guatemalan or a Honduran, when outside his homeland, may allow himself to be called a Central American. But a Costa Rican is always a Costa Rican.

Education and culture are national icons. A sense of what is proper and of the importance of being a well-mannered person are part of the way people live, not merely lessons taught in school. The high rates of literacy and school attendance are facts of life sometimes repeated ad nauseam. Culture in the highbrow

22

sense is a near-mania.

The reason why is one of Costa Rica's mysteries. Only 150 years ago, as the coffee era began, Costa Ricans were just emerging from the era of barefoot, dirt-poor, ignorant backwardness. Not only was there no widespread literacy at the time, there was no national culture, no music, nothing but hard work to survive. Costa Rica's present love of the finer things traces back to the frontier days not at all, except, perhaps, as overcompensation, an obsession with what was once out of reach, and with being a people worthy of relative prosperity.

And how the Costa Ricans have tried to catch up! Long before oil sheiks gave out contracts to raise universities in the desert, Costa Rica invested coffee wealth in crash programs to expand primary education. When opera companies invited from afar had no place to perform, the coffee growers taxed themselves to finance the construction of a national theater to rival any hall in Latin America. When local folk traditions were found to be somewhat pale or even non-existent, the dances and music that were imported with the annexation of Guanacaste province were adopted by all Costa Ricans; the *punto guanacasteco,* performed to the accompaniment of guitar and the xylophone-like gourd marimba became the national dance, and the national folk music became what was played on the quijongo, ocarina and chirimía, a flute, drum and oboe of pre-Columbian origin. Most recently, when President Figueres cast his glance about, and saw that classical music was good but that Costa Ricans were not adept, he arranged for the importation whole of a national orchestra and music school, to be staffed, eventually, by national counterparts in training.

Unlike some notorious opera houses that stand empty in jungles and deserts, the imported elements in the case of Costa Rica were brought to fertile ground and have taken root. A respectable literature includes novels of social realism about exploitation on the banana plantations, and of *costumbrismo,* depicting the everyday happenings and ways of the cities and small towns. Modern and classical composers are appreciated on a broad scale. The best of the visual artists, such as engraver Francisco Amighetti Ruiz, have reached audiences outside of Costa Rica.

Strangely, for a people that has grabbed hold of its destiny and managed it fairly well, Costa Ricans have a strain of fatalism. This is said to come from their Hispanic heritage, and from the churchly lessons of submission and obedience repeated over the years. It also comes out of hundreds of years of poverty that could not be transcended until relatively recently. The values of working hard and bettering oneself predominate, but these don't necessarily go along with planning ahead and being prudent. Costa Ricans are poor savers, and some big-ticket public investments were financed by foreign loans that are now burdensome. But with a sense of limited control over the future, and a past of deprivation, they are consumers *par excellence*. Those who can afford it, and those who can't, eat, drink and dress well, buy all the consumer gadgets they can get their hands on, and enjoy life while they can.

Two minority groups—blacks and Indians—maintain ways different from those of the vast majority of Costa Ricans.

Blacks were present in early colonial Costa Rica in small numbers as slaves, but those who survived the harsh conditions and ill treatment of that era merged into the general population. A later generation of blacks arrived in Costa Rica at the close of the nineteenth century, from Jamaica and elsewhere in the West Indies, to construct the railroad from San José to the Atlantic, and remained to labor on the banana plantations established by Minor Keith.

The newcomers were not welcomed with open arms. Blacks were confined to the coast by a prohibition against spending a night in the Central Valley. But in the lowlands they prospered, taking the best jobs on the plantations, and in commerce in the port of Limón. When Panama disease forced the relocation of the banana industry to the Pacific lowlands in the thirties, many blacks became small farmers, or labored on cacao plantations.

The 30,000 blacks in the country today more and more consider themselves Costa Ricans. All legal discrimination ended with the constitution of 1949. Most blacks who attended school since that time learned Spanish as well as English. Bilingualism has earned some good jobs in commerce and the travel industry in the highlands, though, as Protestants, they stand apart from other Costa Ricans.

24

Indians, or native Americans, are Costa Rica's forgotten minority. Their numbers are few—20,000, perhaps even less—and they live in small groups away from the centers of population.

The original Indian tribes of Costa Rica fragmented and regrouped as a result of war, disease, and exile. The Indians of today range from those whose ways are indistinguishable from those of other Costa Ricans, to jungle groups who have virtually no contact with the outside world.

The Indians of the Talamanca group live in the forested valleys north of the Talamanca mountain range, and in the adjacent Caribbean lowlands. Their ancestors were forced into the area from central Costa Rica and from the Caribbean coast, and there they have remained, except for some who have migrated to the Pacific region. Two tribes survive, the Cabécar and the Bribri, composed of the remnants of a number of pre-Conquest tribes.

For many years, the Talamancan Indians were ruled only nominally from San José, through a native king. As banana operations pushed into their territory, many Talamancans came into regular contact with outsiders; but some of the inland groups remain steadfastly isolated and hostile even to Indians not of their own clan.

The most traditional Talamancan clans are dominated by women, and maintain peculiar customs that include relocating a corpse after a year's burial, isolation of a woman at birth, and relying on native healers.

The Borucas of the southern Pacific coastal area, near Panama, still live largely where they did before the Conquest. Aside from working their land communally, they live like other rural Costa Ricans. But by their racial heritage, their particular devotion to the celebration of the Immaculate Conception, and through pre-Columbian ritual that survives as superstition, the Borucas maintain a separate identity.

Other Indian groups are the Chorotegas of the Nicoya peninsula, who lost the use of their separate language years ago, and are now almost indistinguishable from the mestizo, or mixed-blood, Costa Ricans of the area; and a few Guatusos, who live in the northern border lowlands east of the Guanacaste mountains.

Around Costa Rica

The pages that follow cover the major towns, national parks, beaches and other points of interest in Costa Rica; how to get to them and what you'll find; where to stay, and what you should keep in mind before you go. Of course, not all appropriate travel advice can be repeated for every destination, so you'll also want to read the chapters of practical information at the back of this book before you set out for any place.

Prices are quoted in U. S. dollars, and, in the case of hotels, include the 13 percent room tax. These are subject to change, and should be taken as approximate. You can easily check the latest hotel rates through a travel agent or by calling toll-free U S. numbers, where these are given. Restaurant prices do not include tax and service, which amount to another 20 percent.

Bus, railroad and airplane schedules are, of course, also subject to change. I've given recent schedules to show the ease or difficulty of getting around by public transportation, and to help you plan your time. The tourist office in San José has the latest schedules for public transportation from the capital, or will get them for you. For travel from intermediate points (say, from Nicoya to one of the Pacific beaches), call the hotel where you plan to stay, in order to confirm the latest timetables.

Not all hotels in Costa Rica are listed in this book, but I've tried to give a range, from basic *pensiones* and beach *cabinas* to first-class and luxury establishments. In general, when traveling around Costa Rica, I'd plan to spend the night in towns for which accommodations are listed. Phone ahead for reservations when you can, either directly or through someone else who speaks Spanish. At holidays and on weekends, this will guarantee you a room. At other times, a call will allow the hotel to have

26

your room ready and to lay in supplies—an important factor at some of the beaches where food is not easily available.

Most distances and other measures are given in the metric system, which is now in general use in Costa Rica. Population figures are from the latest official estimates.

Complaints about prices, service or abuses should be addressed to the Costa Rica Tourist Board, Apartado 777, San José, along with proof, if available. I would appreciate having your complaints as well, along with more pleasant discoveries and tidbits of advice that you care to send to me, in care of my publisher.

San José

Population: 305,000; Metropolitan Area Population: 725,000
Altitude: 1182 meters (3877 feet)

San José, the capital of Costa Rica, is many towns. At its center are steel-and-concrete towers, shops with plate-plass windows displaying the latest fashions and consumer electronic gadgetry, thoroughfares busy with traffic, and sidewalks crowded with neatly dressed businessmen and office workers. All might have been transplanted from a medium-sized Spanish city.

Just west of the main square is the bustling market area, much more Central American in character, where tinkerers, wholesalers and vendors of food and every necessity of daily life eke out their livings from tiny shops and market stalls and street stands, where buses and delivery trucks and taxis battle to advance through the throngs and commerce overflowing the sidewalks. Here, the buildings are one- and two-story, relatively dingy, and mostly unseen by the casual observer for all the activity around them.

Farther west of downtown San José, and in some of the surrounding suburbs, are the areas of gracious living, where huddled constructions give way to spacious, ranch-style houses with green lawns, always surrounded by substantial fences. This is where California- and Florida-style living—all the amenities in a benign climate—has grafted itself onto the local scene.

And there are the working-class neighborhoods as well, once-independent villages that lodge in simple, neat and not-unpleasant houses the thousands of people who make San José run.

The city was founded in 1737 as Villa Nueva de la Boca del Monte del Valle de Abra, as the expanding population of the colony of Costa Rica moved westward from Cartago, then the capital. One of dozens of farming centers in a valley of forests, pastures and little plots of subsistence crops, San José—the name of the town was shortened to that of its patron saint—became the capital of Costa Rica during the brief upheavals that followed independence. Only slowly, though, did it grow into a national center, as commerce in coffee and bananas brought substantial revenues to government and business, along with new administrative requirements. But even as San José grew to encompass nearby villages, it never lost its small-town ways. *Josefinos*—the people of the capital—still know most of their neighbors by name, not simply as familiar faces. They shop at the corner store—the *pulpería*—as often as at the supermarket, to pick up the local gossip along with their eggs, coffee and beans. And they gather at *sodas* and bars—their own counterparts of cafés and pubs—to while away spare time and discuss the latest upswings and downturns of their fortunes.

San José sits at the bottom of a teacup valley, the mound-shaped volcano Barva to the north, a ridge of hills to the south, the slopes of both honeycombed with farms. Hardly a part of the city is out of sight of these pastoral surroundings. San José's best moments come in the late afternoon of any day in the rainy season, after a storm has blown through on a near-furious wind, soaked the land, and cooled the air that for an hour or two borders on hot or humid at the coffee altitudes. The sky turns blue again, and wisps of cloud stick to the northern slopes of patchwork fields. As evening falls, clusters of lights turn on in the surrounding higher villages, and twinkle on into the night.

Travelers use San José as a takeoff point for excursions to the many beaches and natural wonders of Costa Rica. Obligatory points of interest are few. But the hotels, country clubs, fine dining, recreational opportunities and measured pace invite the visitor to linger, especially when the weather at home is unpleasantly cold or oppressively hot. Costa Ricans tend to view their capital as a city without a heritage, but I do not think that this is so. For the outsider with time and interest, there are a few fine baroque and Renaissance-style buildings to view, with fantastic turrets and towers, and steep tin roofs, relics of the years of the coffee boom; visits to the magnificent National Theater, and to museums that display the jade and gold and other artistic

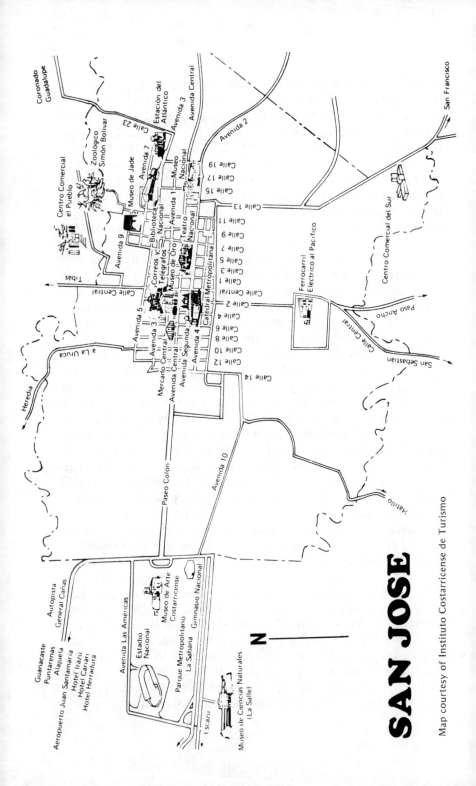

SAN JOSE

Map courtesy of Instituto Costarricense de Turismo

treasures of the nation; plays and concerts to attend, and local ways to observe from the table of a sidewalk café or from the bench of one of the many little parks. The city is low-key, a pleasant place in which to live, and therefore a nice place to visit.

Orientation

Avenidas in San José run from east to west, with odd-numbered avenidas north of Avenida Central, or Central Avenue, and even-numbered avenidas to the south. Calles, or streets, run north-south, with odd-numbered calles east of the Calle Central, even-numbered streets to the west. You'll quickly get used to this scheme as you go around the city, though you'll probably confuse your avenidas and calles at first.

The two main areas of interest to visitors are the central business district, around the intersection of Avenida Central and Calle Central, and the high-toned Paseo Colón district, to the west. Paseo Colón is a continuation of Avenida Central. From the western end of Paseo Colón to the center of the city is just over a mile, a distance easily negotiated on foot or by the many city buses that run along Colón.

Josefinos navigate around their city by inertial displacement from known landmarks. An ad for a certain restaurant might say that it is 200 meters west of and 150 meters north of Edificio Chile Picante. "100 meters" is another way of saying "one block" in Costa Rica (though a block is, in fact, somewhat shorter). The translation, then, is: From the Chile Picante building, go two blocks west, then one-and-a-half blocks north. This system has its charm, and is fine if you know the city, but if you're a first-time visitor, you're sunk. You'll have to seek clarification (e.g., "Where is Edificio Chile Picante?") if you get an address in this form.

Fortunately, a somewhat clearer form is generally used for addresses in the downtown area. The address of the Chalet Suizo restaurant is Avenida 1, Calles 5 y 7. This means that it's on Avenida 1 between 5 and 7 Calles. The address of the Hotel Balmoral is Avenida Central y Calle 7, meaning that it's at the corner of Avenida Central and Calle 7. In this book, I'll give such addresses as "Avenida 1, Calles 5/7," and "Avenida Central, Calle 7." Of course, you'll have to search out the Chalet Suizo restaurant along the block indicated, but that's the way the

Ticos do it.

Believe it or not, buildings also have numbers, but they're rarely posted, so an address giving a house number is of little use.

For obvious reasons, I will not always give addresses and directions in the local manner.

HOTELS

The best hotel values in San José are to be found at the *upper* end of the price scale, but there are also a few good buys in the medium and budget ranges. In general, rooms are larger in the Paseo Colón area than downtown, so you may well give first thought to staying in the west end, at little sacrifice in convenience. Almost all of the budget hotels, however, are downtown.

Reservations are advisable at any holiday period. Take advantage of toll-free telephone numbers for this purpose, if you can. Otherwise, the airport branch of the tourist office will help you find a room in your price range when you arrive.

There are other hotels than those listed below, in outlying areas, but I think that most first-time visitors will want to stay near the central area of San José. For longer visits, consult the ads for furnished apartments in the *Tico Times.*

Better Hotels—West End

Hotel Cariari, Ciudad Cariari, tel. 390022. 160 rooms. $81 single/ $97 double. Mailing address: Apartado 737, Centro Colón, San José.

U. S. reservations: tel. 800-325-1337 + 221 or 800-327-9408.

The Cariari is not in San José at all, but eight kilometers west of the city, along the Cañas expressway, halfway to the airport. This tasteful, modern resort and country-club complex, with its dramatic rotunda entry, has three pools, assorted bars, seafood and steak restaurants, shops, gyms, saunas, whirlpools, an 18-hole golf course, tennis courts, color televisions, air conditioning, car rentals, and many lesser amenities. Shuttle bus service is available to San José for a small charge. The mountain views from the extensive grounds are lovely. I wouldn't blame anybody for spending a whole winter vacation here—nothing is missing. The upper crust of San José society and politics frequents the facilities.

Hotel Sheraton Herradura, Ciudad Cariari, tel. 390033. 120 rooms. $60-90/$65-105. Mailing address: Apartado 7-1880, San José.

U. S. reservations: tel. 800-325-3535.

The Herradura is another large and new hotel, constructed in Spanish colonial style. Rooms are among the nicest in or near San José, and have television and air conditioning. There's a large pool, and guests have access to all the facilities at the Cariari Hotel and Country Club next door. Two good restaurants are located in the hotel, the Swiss Bonanza, a steak house, and the Bon Vivant, which serves French cuisine. And there's even a chapel.

Hotel Irazú, Autopista Gen. Cañas, tel. 324811. 350 rooms. $51/ $59. Mailing address: Apartado 962, San José.

U. S. reservations: tel. 800-327-9408 or 305-588-8541.

The largest hotel in San José, the Irazú is four kilometers west of downtown, on the edge of the city. A modern, low-lying building, it has air-conditioning and t.v. in its rooms, two restaurants (one with good French cuisine), lighted tennis courts, pool, sauna, massage service, and numerous shops and real estate salesmen in its bustling lobby. Shuttle-bus service is provided to downtown.

Hotel Corobici, Calle 42, Avenida 5, tel. 328122. 275 rooms. Mailing address: Apartado 8-5480, San José.

U.S. reservations: 800-325-1337 & 221 or 305-594-1560

A modernesque, cream-colored structure that towers over western San José, the Corobici is under the same management as the Cariari. Excellent facilities include pool, health spa, air conditioning and television, a 24-hour cafeteria as well as restaurant, and a courtesy bus to downtown.

Gran Hotel Costa Rica, Avenida Central, Calle 3, tel. 214000. 104 rooms. $44/$59.

U. S. reservations: tel. 800-327-9408 or 305-588-8541.

Most Central American capitals have a fine, elegant old hotel, and this is San José's. Across from the national theater and fronting on a small park, the Hotel Costa Rica has renovated, modern rooms, all with television, a chandeliered rooftop dining room, and tasteful, sedate public areas. The Parisien Café on the ground floor is a good locale for observing the goings-on in the center of the city.

Hotel Balmoral, Calle 7, Avenida Central, tel. 225022. 140 rooms. **$50/$65.**

U. S. reservations: 800-223-9868 or 212-757-2981. Canada: 800-261-9300.

This is the best of the newer hotels downtown, with good-sized rooms done in modern decor (with air conditioning and t.v.), ample seating in the lobby, a shopping arcade, and even a black-jack casino. The Piccadilly coffee shop is a popular gathering spot.

Hotel Europa, Calle Central, Avenida 5, tel. 221222. 69 rooms. $51/$62.

U. S. reservations: tel. 800-223-6764, 212-758-4375.

A fine traditional hotel, with air-conditioned rooms, television, and the advantage of a pool.

Aurola Holiday Inn, Calle 5, Avenida 5, tel. 337233. 188 rooms. $95/$105. Mailing address: Apartado 7802, 1000 San José.

U. S. reservations: 800-465-4329.

Best-equipped of the downtown hotels, with standard Holiday Inn rooms (which are large for San José), indoor pool, gym, cable television, spa, several bars and restaurants (including the rooftop El Mirador with fine cuisine and unsurpassed views), underground parking, and many shops. Good service, no surprises.

Moderate Hotels, West End

Tennis Club, Sabana Sur (Opposite Metropolitan Park), tel. 321822. 26 rooms. $27-43/$34-50.
This is a fun place to stay, a lively country club with many of the features of the Cariari and Herradura, but in more modest quarters. Guests have use of tennis courts, pools, sauna, bowling alley and billiard tables, with some restrictions. The restaurant has a limited but reasonably priced menu. No shops or travel services here.

Hotel Torremolinos, Avenida 5 bis, Calle 40, tel. 225266. 73 rooms. $56/$63
In a nice residential neighborhood not far from the Paseo Colón, modest rooms, pool.

Hotel Ambassador, Paseo Colón, Calle 28, tel. 218155. 70 rooms. $29-42/$37-50.
Plain, good-sized rooms. Italian restaurant with limited service.

Apartotel Napoleón, Calle 40, Avenida 5, tel. 233252. 32 units. $26-32/$33-40.
This is a hotel of housekeeping units consisting of large bedrooms with attached kitchenettes. Good location, not far from Paseo Colón. Rooms have t.v. and air conditioning, and there's a pool. This and the other "apartoteles" listed below are the best value in San José, if you don't need the shops, travel agency and room service provided by conventional hotels.

Apartotel Castilla, Calle 24, Avenidas 2/4, tel. 222113. 25 units. $30/$45.
More modest than the Napoleón on the outside, but the units, with one and two bedrooms, are comfortable. Near Paseo Colón.

Apartotel Ramgo, Sabana Sur (two blocks south of Metropolitan Park), tel. 223823. $34 double, $40 triple. Mailing address: Apartado 1441, San José.
Plain but large apartments with terraces in a residential area on the western edge of San José.

Moderate Hotels, Downtown

I'm sorry to say that most downtown hotels in this category are more moderate in their facilities than in their prices. Most appear to have been sliced from the same modern office cube, according to the size of the available lot, and set down in place. All have limited public space—usually a couple of chairs and sofas in a miniature lobby—and would fit more appropriately in the crowded confines of Amsterdam. Some, indeed, have Dutch names. Don't shy away from these establishments if you want to stay in the middle of the downtown action, but don't expect more than a modest room, either.

Hotel Royal Dutch, Calle Central, Avenida Central, tel. 221414. 58 rooms. $44 single/$59 double. Mailing address: Apartado 4258, San José.

U. S. reservations: tel. 800-223-6764 or 212-758-4375.

Air-conditioned rooms with television, well-managed. The restaurant is good, with a fixed lunch for $4 to $6, and an Indonesian combination plate on Wednesdays. Furnished apartments are also available at a nearby downtown location.

Hotel Plaza, Av. Central, Calle 2/4, tel. 225533. 40 rooms. $20/$26. Mailing address: Apartado 2019, San José.

Central location, restaurant and bar, carpeted airy rooms.

Hotel Amstel, Calle 7, Avenida 1, tel. 224622. 55 rooms. $23-37/$31-42. Mailing address: Apartado 4192, San José.

Air-conditioned rooms in various sizes, less claustrophobic than other downtown hotels, well-run, with good and reasonably priced food. Nice location just off Morazán Park.

Hotel La Gran Vía, Av. Central, Calles 1/3, tel. 227737. 32 rooms. $23/$27.

The usual tiny lobby, small rooms, some of which are air-conditioned and have balconies for watching the action on Avenida Central. Restaurant.

Hotel Presidente, Avenida Central, Calles 7/9, tel 223022. 47 rooms. $20-32/$27-37.

Some rooms air conditioned, basic restaurant, bar.

Hotel Talamanca, Avenida 2, Calles 8/10, tel. 335033. 56 rooms. $22/$25. Mailing address: Apartado 449, San José.

Located in the noisy bus terminal and market area. Some rooms have t.v. Restaurant, bar.

Apartamentos Lamm, Calle 15, Av. 1, tel. 214920. 19 units. $26-56/$30-60.

Basic housekeeping units with t.v. in a nice location off National Park.

Apartotel San José, Avenida 2, Calle 17/19, tel. 220455. 14 units. $23-28/$28-34.

Similar to Apartamentos Lamm, in a more commercial area.

Hotel Galilea, Av. Central, Calles 11/13, tel. 336925. 24 rooms. $17/$20.

Modern and plain, fair value, near the bus for Cartago, otherwise not a good location.

Budget Hotels

Hotel Ritz, Calle Central, Av. 8/10, tel. 224103. 16 rooms. $11/$16.

A modest hotel with small, plain, but clean rooms, and the special asset of warm, helpful American owners. Doubles have private bath. Breakfast only served ($1 and up), coffee on the house, reading area. Upstairs.

Petit Hotel, Calle 24 No. 39. 12 rooms. $10-15/$15-26.

A converted private home, with rooms far more ample and light and airy than at budget hotels downtown. Excellent location one-half block south of Paseo Colón, within walking distance of most intercity buses. Friendly, good value. The lower rates are without private bath.

Hotel Don Carlos, Calle 9, Avenidas 7/9, tel. 216707. 10 rooms. $25/$30. Mailing address: Apartado 1593, 1000 San José.

A good smaller hotel in a converted private house, with comfortable, renovated rooms. Centrally located on a quiet street. Rates include light breakfast. Apartments available for about $200 per week.

Costa Rica Inn, Calle 9, Avenidas 1/3, tel. 225203. 15 rooms. $12/$18.

Tidy and homey, on a quiet street near the city center. All rooms with private bath, and all suffering from the budget-hotel blues of San José: little light and ventilation. But a relatively good value. Rates slightly lower by the week.

The above hotels are the best of the budget establishments in San José. The remainder are listed without particular enthusiasm.

Hotel-Soda Poás, Avenidas 7, Calles 3/5. $4 per person.

Basic, small rooms, clean, a favorite of travelers despite such occasional problems as animals in the walls.

Hotel Astoria, Avenida 7, Calles 7/9, tel 212174. $4 per person.

Basic, clean.

Pension Villa Blanca, Avenida 7, Calles 2/4. $3 per person.

Older, plain and musty, but, as they say, honorable.

Hotel América, 7 Avenida, Calles 2/4, tel. 214116. $4/$6.

Newer, basic.

Hotel Central, Avenida 3, Calles 6/8. $8/$12.

Small rooms, in bus terminal-market area.

Hotel Johnson, Calle 8, Avenidas Central /2, tel. 237633. $8/$11.

Relatively large rooms with private bath, near bus terminal and market.

Gran Hotel Centroamericano, Avenida 2, Calles 6/8, tel. 213362. 50 rooms, $7-11/$13-19.

Rank after rank of small rooms, no exterior windows, prison-like. Rooms with musty carpeting cost more.

Hotel Boston, Avenida 8, Calles Central /2, tel. 210563. $9/$13.

Older establishment with larger rooms than most in the budget range.

Hotel Park, Avenida 4, Calles 2/4, tel. 216944. $17/$25.

Large, dark rooms. The bar here is popular with visitors.

Hotel Canadá, Avenida 5, Calles 6/8. $1.50 per person.

Flophouse-type cubicles.

Hotel Asia, Calle 11, Avenidas Central /1, tel. 233893. $4/$8.

Simple, with tiny rooms and little light, but clean. Chinese-run, as you might guess. Upstairs.

Camping
The only trailer park currently operating near San José is in San Antonio de Belén, eight kilometers west of the city. Take the San Antonio exit from the Cañas expressway, and follow the signs to the trailer park. Rates are $5 per day with full hook-up, less without.

RESTAURANTS

Some very good food, indeed, is to be found in and near San José. Numerous restaurants specialize in Swiss, Central European, Spanish, French, Italian and Chinese cuisine, as well as steaks and seafood. There are many clean, reasonably priced luncheonettes, and a very few restaurants even serve native Costa Rican specialties.

The best chefs take advantage of the beef, fish (usually corvina, or sea bass), chicken and fresh fruits and vegetables that are abundant at all times of the year. Shrimp and lobster are usually available and are attractively served in a number of restaurants, but are no bargain. Drinkable wines and imported liquors are quite expensive—double or triple the American price—so you may want to consider the excellent Costa Rican beers or local rums and other spirits.

Most restaurants open for lunch from 11:30 a.m. to 2:30 p.m., and for dinner from 6:30 p.m. or 7 p.m. to 10 or 10:30 p.m. Luncheonettes ("sodas") and many of the inexpensive restaurants are open throughout the day. A good dinner hour in San José is 7:30 p.m. or so.

My selection of restaurants is mostly limited to the downtown and Paseo Colón areas, near the major hotels. There are many more good choices, both in these neighborhoods and in the suburbs. Consult the ads in the *Tico Times* and the *Grapevine Tourist Guide*.

Downtown

Chalet Suizo, Avenida 1, Calles 5/7. The Swiss Chalet is nicely atmospheric, with wainscotted walls, wooden beams, brick hearth and costumed waiters. And the cuisine is authentic. The house steak, covered with ham and cheese, is excellent, and there are fondues, goulash, smoked pork chops, seafood items, fine French and Italian desserts, and much more. Most entrees run $4 to $6.

Isle de France, Calle 7, Avenidas Central /2. An excellent little French restaurant. Not at all cheap for San José. A daily complete lunch goes for about $10. Specialties are paté maison, smoked ham, Vichyssoise, snails, sea bass on spinach, and steak au poivre. Most entrees $6 and up.

Casino Español, Calle 7, Avenidas Central /7. The gastronomic tour continues with fine Spanish cuisine. Specialties are quail in wine, tripe, Asturian fabada (stew), and paella. Elegant atmosphere and service. Entrees from $8.

Probably no city in the hemisphere has as many Chinese eateries for its size as San José. Chinese food generally runs in the medium price range. And you pay extra for rice. A selection of three from the bounty:

Lung Mun, Avenida 1, Calles 5/7. Good Cantonese food, plus a variety of Costa Rican beef and fish entrees, all in the $3-to-$5 range. Open throughout the day.

Fulusu, Calle 7, Avenidas Central /2. One of the better Chinese restaurants. Chow mein and such for $4, more elaborate shrimp and fish entrees for $9 and up.

Fortuna, Avenida 6, Calles 2/4. The specialty is Manchurian cuisine, along with the usual pork, chicken and fish dishes, at $3 to $6 for an entree. Lobster in season in a variety of preparations, $14. I liked number 54.

La Hacienda, Calle 7, Avenidas Central /2. One of many restaurants in San José specializing in charcoal-broiled steaks and chops, but one of the few downtown. Dinner is $5 to $7, weekday luncheon specials are less.

Escorial, Avenidas 1, Calles 5/7. A popular, popular-priced, noisy, open-to-the-street restaurant that might have been transplanted from the bullring district of Seville, music and all. Daily changing luncheon combinations for 50 cents (yes) to $1.50, served from 11 a.m. to 2 p.m., and many, many Spanish specialties—eight kinds of paella, Spanish sausage, Asturian stew, mixed grills and seafood platters, mostly in the $4-to-$6 range. Breakfast also served.

La Cosina de Leña. You could spend weeks in San José and think that native-style food didn't exist. La Cosina de Leña (The Wood Stove), in the El Pueblo shopping center north of downtown, is one of the few places where you can enjoy home cooking. Tiny tables, piles of firewood, whitewashed walls, subdued lighting, and decorations of colorful enamelware and gourd beakers all re-create the atmosphere of a dark, smoky country kitchen. The menu—printed on a paper bag—is a lesson in traditional Costa Rican cooking. Some items: olla de carne (meat stew), mondongo en salsa (ox in tomato sauce), stuffed pepper or cabbage, chilasquiles (tortillas filled with meat), pozol (corn soup), and the old standby, gallo pinto (rice and beans). Most entrees are served with tortillas and beans, and run $3 to $4. To get here take the Calle Blancos bus from Calle 1, Avenidas 3/5.

Also in El Pueblo are **Lancer's Steak House,** which offers complete, low-priced lunches; and **Rías Bajas,** an excellent seafood house.

Cafés: There aren't many of these, but two are reminiscent of Europe. The Parisien Café of the Hotel Costa Rica, Calle 3 at Avenida 2, provides sidewalk seating with a view to the national theater, the Plaza de la Cultura, and the adjacent small park. A fine place for extended sitting, reading or people-watching. More elegant is the café across the street in the National Theater itself where, at marble-topped tables, surrounded by works of art and bathed in recorded chamber music, you can enjoy a sandwich and coffee for less than $2.

Buffets: The Hotel Balmoral, Avenida Central at Calle 7, offers a buffet on weekdays from 11 a.m. to 2 p.m. in its second-floor restaurant. There's usually a stew, a chicken dish, pasta and salad. Plain, but filling for $4. On Mondays, Wednesdays and Fridays, the Hotel Costa Rica, Avenida Central at Calle 3, serves a buffet lunch in its ground-floor Jardín restaurant for $4.25, dessert and coffee included.

Sodas are San José's all-purpose coffee shops and diners, where in simple, soda-shop surroundings you can enjoy anything from a cup of coffee or a drink to a sandwich or a steak. At Soda Sina, opposite the Hotel Amstel at Calle 7 and Avenida 1, complete breakfasts are about $2, shots of rum 80 cents, main meat and fish courses $2.50 to $3. Similar fare and clean surroundings are available at almost any soda in San José. Among them are:

Soda Central, Avenida 1, Calles 3/5. A hole in the wall with cheap sandwiches and drinks.

Soda Palace, Avenida 2, Calle 2, on Parque Central. Good seats for watching the main square.

Fast Food: McDonald's, familiar and reliable, is at Calle 4, Avenidas Central /1. Prices are about the same as in the States, and they have refreshing iced tea with lemon. Another location on Calle 42, a couple of blocks south of Paseo Colón. Pollo Kentucky (Kentucky Fried Chicken), has outlets at Avenida 2 and Calle 6, Avenida Central and Calle 2, and Paseo Colón, Calles 32/34. The colonel's lunch runs $2 to $3. Last and not so fast is Pizza Hut, serving pizzas, subs and spaghetti at Avenida 1, Calles 3/5; Calle 4, Avenidas Central /2; and Paseo Colón at Calle 28.

Snacks: Pops, Avenida Central, Calles 1/3 (and just about everywhere else in San José) has the best ice cream in Costa Rica. Pastelería Schmidt, Avenida 2 at Calle 4, sells excellent breads and pastries, which may be eaten in, with a cup of coffee, or carried out. Another location at Avenida Central and Calle 11. San José's ubiquitous fruit carts sell bananas and pineapple and papaya at almost every corner. At Christmas, they offer apples and grapes, which are great and expensive delicacies. And there are many hamburger and hot dog vendors as well.

West End

Club Londres, Paseo Colón at Calle 40, tel. 227896. Fine, creative continental dining, some of the best in San José. Delicate sauces, crisp vegetables, faultless service and presentation. Among the many fine selections: sea bass with raisins or in mustard sauce, tenderloin tips in sauce (this is the kind of meat even non-beefeaters like), tournedos. Main courses $7 and up. Reservations advised.

La Bastille, Paseo Colón at Calle 22, is a fine French restaurant, where food preparation is painstaking. A changing menu takes advantage of the best available ingredients. $10 and up.

Lobster's Inn, Paseo Colón at Calle 24. Good seafood. Lobster and shrimp are expensive—$17—but sea bass (corvina) is reasonable at about $6, served in a variety of ways.

Ana, Paseo Colón, Calles 24/26. An unpretentious and inexpensive Italian restaurant serving lasagna, spaghetti, veal and non-Italian dishes for $3 to $5. Pleasant surroundings. Try the upstairs dining room.

El Chicote, Sabana Norte (facing the north side of, and near the west end of, Metropolitan Park). An excellent steak house with a nice arched interior, and reasonable prices. All sorts of steaks and chops go for $4 to $6.50, and a few creative specialties, such as tenderloin stuffed with shrimp, are $10 and up. To get here, take the bus marked "Sabana Estadio" from Avenida 3 between Calles Central and 1, or from along Paseo Colón.

Swiss Bonanza, Hotel Herradura. Excellent assortment of filets, chops and sea bass, all surprisingly reasonable at $5 and up, with salad bar. Drive out, or take the Alajuela microbus (from Calle 14, Avenidas 1/3).

Soda Tapia, Calle 42, Avenida 2, opposite Metropolitan Park. More a cafe than a soda, good for sandwiches and fruit salad at the outdoor tables. Also at Colón, Calles 32/34.

44

Bars

Drinking is a pastime that most Costa Ricans feel comfortable with, and the visitor, in turn, will feel comfortable in any half-way-decent-looking bar. All are reasonably priced, with domestic drinks for $1 or less. Bocas (snacks) are served on the side. Many of the downtown bars are good places to rendezvous with other foreigners. Among them:

Ye Pub, Calle Central, Avenida 7. Sort of English.

New York Bar, Avenida 1, Calles 7/9.

Disco Túnel del Tiempo, Avenida Central, Calles 7/9 (A discotheque, not a bar, but centrally located.)

Key Largo, Calle 7, Avenida 3, on Morazán Park. Nice, old house with a few nautical motifs in the yard and Tiffany lamps in one of the dark drinking rooms, not quite the Bogart atmosphere that the management advertises.

THE SIGHTS OF SAN JOSE

San José does not have all that much in the way of obligatory sights to see. If your time is short, limit your rounds to the high points: the National Theater and Plaza of Culture, the National Museum, and the Jade Museum. These can be seen in a half day, or between excursions to the volcanoes and countryside around San José. At a more leisurely pace, you can cover the itinerary below, and get to know the city better, in a couple of days or more. Most of the places mentioned are within a half-mile or so of the Central Park.

Any walking tour of San José starts at the Parque Central (the Central Park, or main square), bounded by Calles Central and 2, and Avenidas 2 and 4. Bus after city bus stops and accepts the long queues of commuters along all four edges. Horns beep incessantly and traffic slams into gear and races ahead at the change of lights on wide Avenida 2. Office buildings and advertising billboards tower overhead. But the park is an oasis in all this, a neat, gardened square where workers on their breaks and anyone with a few moments to spare will sit on the benches, pass

Central San José

the time of day, read a book, and, perhaps, engage the visitor in conversation about such favorite themes as Costa Rican democracy, Costa Rican economic problems, Costa Rican foreign policy, and Costa Rican women. A massive bandstand squats at the center of the park, sheltering a children's library in its base. Public concerts are offered on most Sunday mornings in this musically concerned city.

Across Calle Central from the park is the Catedral Metropolitana (Metropolitan Cathedral), one of the many undistinguished churches of relatively recent vintage in San José. Cream-colored, blocky on the outside, with neo-classical pediment and columns at the entry, the Cathedral has a massive, barrel-arched interior. Much more interesting is the ecclesiastical administration building attached to the rear of the Cathedral, done in the charming and disappearing nineteenth-century San José style, with a European face—in this instance stone-cased windows and pediments straight out of Renaissance Italy—and a red tin roof.

A couple of blocks down Avenida 2, at the corner of Calle 3, is the Teatro Nacional, the National Theater, which over the years has come to embody San José and its self-image as a cultural center. And with good reason, for a more impressive public structure is to be found in no city for a thousand miles to the north or south.

The construction of the theater came about in a fit of national pique, after an opera company cancelled a performance in San José in 1890, for lack of a suitable hall. In response, the coffee growers of Costa Rica levied a cultural tax on their exports, engaged the appropriate experts, and had their theater completed seven years after the insult.

Though sometimes advertised as a replica of the Paris or Milan opera, the block-long National Theater is neither, and stands on its own. Columns and pediment and window arches are carved into the massive stone blocks of its majestic neo-classical facade, which is crowned with allegorical statues of Dance, Music and Fame. The sides of the building are less elegant, faced with cement plaster, and the tin roofing is purely San José.

Astride the entrance to the theater stand statues of Beethoven and the Spanish dramatist Calderón de la Barca; in the vestibule are allegorical figures of Comedy and Tragedy. In the Costa Rican tradition of importing and assimilating Culture, these were executed by European masters. Belgians designed the building and fabricated its steel structural members. And Germans, Spaniards and Italians collaborated on the architectural work and interior decoration. But Costa Rica is present as well. The sculpture called Heroes of Misery, in the vestibule, is the work of native Juan Ramón Bonilla; and the stairway paintings depict themes of Costa Rican life and commerce—coffee and banana harvest and shipment, and local fruits and flowers. The parquet flooring in much of the theater is made from native hardwoods.

Especially impressive inside the theater building are the foyer, upstairs, with its three-part ceiling painting representing Dawn, Day and Night; the interior marble staircases; the gilt decorations throughout; and, of course, the multitiered great hall.

The National Theater is the locale of regular concerts by the national orchestra, which was transformed into a full-time professional and teaching organization in 1971, with the acquisition of a number of foreign musicians; and of performances by the youth orchestra, and native and foreign drama companies and artists. Tickets are sold in advance at the little building alongside the theater. Admission for sightseeing costs 50 cents.

National Theater and Plaza of Culture

Opposite the entrance to the National Theater is a little park where vendors of handicrafts—model oxcarts, dolls, jewelry and leather—display their wares on Sundays. Adjacent is the stately Gran Hotel Costa Rica, with its pleasant ground-floor café. There's another café in the theater itself.

Along Avenida Central between Calles 3 and 5 is the Plaza de la Cultura (Plaza of Culture). The commercial buildings that once occupied the site were razed to create an open expanse decorated with flowers and benches, and platforms where outdoor performances are sometimes given. To preserve the broad vista to the adjacent National Theater, a complex of exhibit halls has been constructed below ground level. Foremost of the displays is the exquisite gold collection of the Banco Central de Costa Rica, with over a thousand pre-Columbian decorations, mostly from burial sites in the southern Pacific coastal region of Costa Rica. Also included are jade ornaments from Costa Rica and other countries.

Near the entrance to the exhibit area, at the corner of Avenida Central and Calle 5, is the information center of the Costa Rican Tourist Board (Instituto Costarricense de Turismo), where the personnel are quite helpful in answering questions, providing maps, schedules and brochures, and generally orienting the visitor. Adjacent to the tourist office, facilities are provided for cashing travelers checks on weekend mornings.

Six blocks east of the Plaza of Culture, and up the hill known as the Cuesta de Moras, is the National Museum (Museo Nacional), housed in the old Bellavista Fortress, once the headquarters of the now-defunct army.

Of major interest in the museum is the pre-Columbian collection, one of the largest of its kind. All of the materials are shown quite logically, divided into the three major cultural zones of the country, and arranged chronologically for each. Many but not all of the exhibits are labelled in both English and Spanish, and a map helps to explain Costa Rica's importance as a meeting point of three cultural traditions. It's fascinating to see in a few minutes the progress of pottery in the Nicoya region, over a period of more than a thousand years, from plain and primitive figurines to the exquisite polychrome vases in anthropomorphic form that were manufactured at the time of the Spanish conquest. In the Atlantic region, the figures are less sophisticated, in buff and brown, but no less beautiful. The Diquis region is represented by its own pottery styles, and by its fabled, near-perfect stone spheres, some of which are up to two-and-a-half meters in diameter. There are, as well, examples of goldwork, including pendants and pectoral discs, and jade from the northern half of Costa Rica.

The National Museum also has an extensive collection of colonial furniture; printing presses and historical imprints from the era of independence; period costumes; portraits of presidents and politicians; and a cellar of religious art, including saints in wood and plaster, vestments, and paintings executed over the period from colonial times to the present.

Bellavista fortress itself is one of the few colonial-style structures in San José, dominating the central part of the city, massive, towered, gray and brusque on the outside, pocked by bullet holes from the 1948 civil war, but quite lovely from the inner gardened courtyard, with tile roofs, whitewashed walls, and covered passageways. All of the exhibit rooms have high, beamed ceilings. On sale at the museum shop are examples of Talamanca Indian weaving, bows and arrows, and gourd crafts, which

Nicoya Pottery in National Museum

are some of the best souvenirs available in San José.

The National Museum is open every day except Monday from 9:30 a.m. to 5 p.m. There is a small admission charge.

Facing the north side of the National Museum, across Avenida Central, is the Legislative Assemby, a cream-colored, Moorish-style building. You may go in the side door and look around, but it's all quite unprepossessing and uninteresting, except, perhaps, as an artifact of Costa Rica's rather un-Latin non-aggrandizement of its political institutions. North of the legislature is Parque Nacional (National Park), one of San José's nicely landscaped shady squares. The city planners have gone in for tall trees that make for a wonderful cool shade in the middle of the day. The park's centerpiece is an allegorical statue depicting the five Central American nations in arms, driving out the American adventurer William Walker, who had installed himself as ruler of Nicaragua in 1856. Across from the north side of the park is the National Library (Biblioteca Nacional), a modern and not particularly attractive airline-terminal sort of building, decorated with a splotchy mosaic of the sun. There are exhibit areas inside.

Northwest of National Park is the block-square compound of

50

the National Liquor Factory. Liquor is a big business in Costa Rica, in terms of the size of the country, and most of it is the business of the government-owned factory.

West of the liquor factory, between Avenidas 5 and 7, at 11 Calle, is Parque España (Park of Spain), also known as Parque de la Expresión, an enchanting little enclave of towering tropical trees transplanted from around the country. On Sundays, many of San José's artists display and sell their work here.

On the north side of Parque España, at Avenida 7 and Calle 11, is the modern office tower of the Instituto Nacional de Seguros, the government insurance monopoly. On the eleventh floor is the Museum of Pre-Columbian Jade (Museo de Jade), open every day except Monday from 8 a.m. to 5 p.m. The name of the museum is somewhat misleading, for the collection is extensive, with contemporary pottery, tools, weapons and dress of the surviving native peoples of Costa Rica; exhibits showing how jade and gold and stone were worked; and a fascinating assortment of utilitarian art, with such pieces as metates (grinding stones) in anthropomorphic form. Of course, there is much purely decorative art, including jade pendants and necklaces produced by cultures that have now been obliterated.

The museum also offers from its high perch some excellent views of San José and environs—to the north and the volcanoes from the lounge, and to the south and the city center from the vestibule. The first building visible to the south is the Edificio Metálico (Metal Building), an unusual structure designed in France by Victor Baltard, architect of Les Halles. Incongruous and green-painted, with now-rusting roof panels, the Edificio Metálico was one of the first of the pre-fabs, shipped in pieces from Europe. It's now used as a school.

Across Calle 11 from the insurance building is the attractive, Spanish-style Casa Amarilla, which houses Costa Rica's foreign ministry.

North of Parque España is one of the more traditional neighborhoods of San José. Here are large, older homes in wood, decorated with fretwork and crowned with steep tin roofs; and stuccoed brick homes with Renaissance and baroque elements, sometimes painted in pastel colors. See this tropical wedding-cake architecture while you can. Construction in San José has ground almost to a halt recently, but these buildings are sure to disappear.

At the northern edge of downtown is Parque Zoológico Simón Bolívar (Simón Bolívar Zoological Park). Follow Calle 7 north, then Avenida 11 east to the entrance. Here are turtles, monkeys, macaws, peccaries, vultures, jaguars, alligators, ducks, and much else brought from all parts of Costa Rica to a rain forest planted in the middle of the city, complete with palms, bromeliads and aromatic plants. The zoo is well worth a visit if you have even a mild interest in the wildlife of Costa Rica. Also here are the offices of Cida, an environmental information center where publications about the national parks are on sale. Bolívar Park is open from 9 a.m. to 3:30 p.m. (to 4:30 p.m. on weekends), with a small admission charge.

South of the zoo, back in the central part of the city, is Parque Morazán (Morazán Park), divided by heavily trafficked Calle 7 and Avenida 3 into four separate gardens. The nicest is the Japanese-style northeast section, with ponds, a temple-like gazebo, little bridges, and a kids' playground. The structure at the center of the park is the Temple of Music, another of San José's tributes to the finer things.

West along Avenida 3, between Calles Central and 1, is the United States embassy. In many other Latin American capitals, embassies have moved from the decaying and shabby downtown core to elegant districts on the outskirts. Not so in San José, where downtown remains viable, vibrant, and frequented by all the social classes of the metropolitan area. The embassy is one of the more common reference points for giving directions in San José.

Farther west, on Avenida 1 between Calles Central and 2, is the elegant shell of the old Club Unión, where the upper strata of Costa Rican society gathered, until a fire did in the facilities. Just across Calle 2, facing a pleasant mini-park, is the baroque palace that houses the central post office (Correos y Telégrafos, or Cortel).

The Central Market (Mercado Central), at Calle 6 and Avenida 1, is a block-square area housing vendors of flowers, baskets, vegetables, shoes, spices, and a few souvenirs. It's small and sedate by Central American standards, but worth a walk-through. Other markets nearby are the Borbón, a block north, at Calle 8 between

Avenidas 3 and 5, and the Coca-Cola bus terminal and market, Calle 16 between Avenidas 1 and 3. Just as interesting as the markets is the thriving general commerce of the area, where stores, stalls and street hustlers hawk fruit, firecrackers, flypaper, firearms, and countless other articles, many of which you'd have trouble finding at home.

One last downtown reference point, bounded by Avenidas 2 and 4 and Calles 12 and 14, is Parque Carrillo (Carrillo Park), also known as Parque Merced, after the church nearby. The park is typically treed and nicely landscaped, though the neighborhood is heavily trafficked and noisy. One interesting feature, though, is the park's centerpiece, a four-foot-diameter pre-Columbian stone sphere from Palmar Sur, in the southern Diquis region. Other examples of these near-perfect forms are to be seen at the National Museum and, as originals or reproductions, on many a lawn in San José, where they are popular decorations.

North of downtown, and of interest to visitors with time to browse and shop, is the El Pueblo Shopping Center (Centro Comercial). This is a tasteful, charming collection of shops, offices and restaurants, constructed in a style reminiscent of a colonial village, with narrow lanes, wrought-iron lamps, tile roofs, whitewashed brick and stuccoed walls, and beamed ceilings. It's almost better than the real thing. Take the Calle Blancos bus from Calle 1, Avenidas 3/5, to get to El Pueblo.

Less than a mile to the west of downtown, at the opposite end of the upscale Paseo Colón district, is Parque Metropolitano (Metropolitan Park), or La Sabana, once the airport for San José. A drained lake has been restored, trees have grown back, and extensive sport facilities have been erected, including a pool, gymnasium, and stadium.

On the east side of the park, facing Paseo Colón, is the former airport control tower, now converted to the Museo de Arte Costarricense (Museum of Costa Rican Art). Most of the paintings reflect an appreciation of the bucolic and the archaic that contrasts with modern Costa Rican life. Frequent subjects and motifs are idealized landscapes, Indian cultures long gone from the land, and oxcarts and whitewashed adobe houses; in other words, the simple life. Of the works displayed, Francisco Amighetti's woodcuts have earned the most fame outside of Costa Rica. The museum is open every day except Monday from 10 a.m. to 4:30 p.m., and there is a small admission charge. Any Sabana bus from Avenida 3, Calles Central /2, or from the Central Park, will stop near the entrance.

The Museo de Ciencias Naturales (Natural Sciences Museum), is located near the southwest corner of La Sabana park, in the La Salle High School. The collection includes over a thousand stuffed birds, monkeys, and other denizens of the wild, many in mock-ups of their natural habitats. The museum is open during school hours, 9 a.m. to 3 p.m., Monday through Friday from March to November, with a small admission charge. Buses from the Central Park marked "Sabana Cementerio" stop nearby.

The high point of San José for visitors interested in insects will be the Museo de Entomología (Entomology Museum) at the University of Costa Rica. The butterfly collection is especially good. Hours are from 1 p.m. to 6 p.m. on Wednesday and Thursday only. Take a San Pedro bus from the Central Park.

After you've been in San José for a few days, you'll get some sense of the character of the city—progressive and relatively prosperous, but not ostentatious; fast-paced, but not frenetic; well-mannered and neat, but friendly and not excessively formal; respectful of tradition, but with few visible reminders of the past; a national capital, a center of commerce, but manageable in size; a collection of well-off and middling and working-class neighborhoods, with few areas of grinding poverty or ostentatious luxury. One says "but" and "not quite" rather often in describing San José, and all of Costa Rica, the country that has been called the "land of the happy medium."

But despite the progress of the last century, so evident in the efficient functioning of the capital, the crowds of customers at shops and restaurants, and the dense traffic, the economic crisis of recent years has dealt a severe blow to Costa Rica and its self-image. The nation now teeters on the brink of re-entry into the less privileged ranks of the third world. The unemployment rate has regularly been 10 percent or higher. Purchasing power has shrunken following the devaluation of the currency. Fully 70 percent of Costa Rican families, according to official figures, have incomes below the poverty line, locally defined as $100 per month.

And yet, the hard figures are not reflected in San Jose's sur-

54

face. The middle class struggles to maintain its style and good taste, even with limited funds. Josefinos are generally well groomed; their clothes are fashionable, though their wardrobes are limited. Their automobiles are small, but well maintained. Straitened elegance is the style, and it's catching. One diplomat currently may be spotted tooling around San José in a tiny Renault with a uniformed chauffeur.

One of the great debates into which visitors are drawn has to do with the merits of Costa Rica's women, and especially those of San José, who have acquired an extra-regional reputation for their beauty and charm. At the risk of sounding blasé, I will join the controversy and say that there are as many good-looking women in other places as well. But Ticas (and Ticos as well) are generally well groomed and well dressed, and in better shape than most Americans. And their preference for clothing that appears to have been pasted onto their bodies only enhances their fame (and form).

To a casual observer, San José appears to have a high Jewish population. Many a neck is adorned by a gold or silver star of David. In fact, the star has acquired a certain cachet as a pop symbol among Catholic Costa Ricans—quite a difference from other Latin American nations, where swastikas are frequently seen.

Another difference that you'll notice, if you read Spanish, is in the newspapers. Editorials freely criticize the government, and names of junketing legislators are published for the enlightenment of their constituents. Elsewhere in Latin America, the authorities of the day are treated with kid gloves.

The liveliest time of year in San José is the month-long celebration that starts on December 1. Avenida Central is closed to traffic earlier and earlier in the day. Chinamos, stalls selling such seasonal goodies as apples and grapes, toys, and the makings of nativity scenes, crowd the sidewalks. Merchants open their businesses through the midday hours and even on weekends. The throngs grow larger and larger and louder and louder, and drunker and rowdier. Christmas is just a short pause in the round of parades, dancing, bonhomie, confetti-tossing and general street partying that bursts finally at New Year's and dissolves into the traditional mass hangover. The start of this orgy of self-indulgence coincides not with any religious or civic anniversary, but with the day when the aguinaldo, the yearly bonus for salaried employees, is usually paid.

SAN JOSE DIRECTORY

Airport

Juan Santamaría International Airport is located on the outskirts of Alajuela, 17 kilometers west of San José. It's a small and manageable facility serving both domestic and foreign scheduled flights. Local charter flights use the smaller airfield at Pavas, nearer to San José.

Passengers arriving at the airport will come to the tourist information counter before passing through the customs check. Make reservations here for a hotel in town if you don't already have one arranged, and pick up any other information you need—they're quite helpful. To change money, you'll have to go left and back inside the terminal building after you leave the customs area. Banking hours are Monday to Saturday from 7 a.m. to 5 p.m., Sunday from 10 a.m. to 1 p.m. It's a good idea to change a substantial amount at the airport to avoid the long lines at banks in town.

Transport from the airport to San José is available by taxi for $8; by collective microbus for less than 50 cents; and by the regular Alajuela-San José buses and microbuses that stop in front of the terminal. Fare on these is about 25 cents, but luggage space is limited.

To get to the airport from San José, take the Alajuela microbus from Calle 14, Avenidas 1/3 or the bus from Calle 12, Avenidas 3/5; a taxi; or call Blanco Travel Service at **221792** to arrange to share a taxi.

When you depart Costa Rica by air, you may purchase only 50 American dollars at the bank—if they have the cash available. First check in with your airline and pay the exit tax, which is currently $8 (though there has been talk of raising it to $20!). The usual assortment of overpriced airport shops solicits your last Costa Rican coins. The post office branch is open until 5 p.m. The duty-free shop, located beyond the immigration post in the departure area, has a good assortment of liquor, cigarettes and perfumes, and some odds and ends of other luxury goods.

All items are priced in even U. S. dollar amounts (Costa Rican currency is accepted as well), and you may carry your purchases out the door.

Airlines

Scheduled service to San José is currently provided by:

LACSA, Costa Rica's international airline, Calle 1, Avenida 5, tel. 310033; airport, tel. 416244.

SANSA, the domestic airline, Calle 24, Avenidas Central /1, tel. 333258.

Challenge International, Calle 1, Avenida 5, tel. 221166.

Eastern Airlines, Paseo Colón, Calles 26/28, tel. 225655.

Aeronica, Calle 1, Avenida 2, tel. 332483; airport, tel. 416094.

SAM (Colombia), Avenida 5, Calles 1/3, tel. 333066.

COPA (Panama), Calle 1, Avenida 5, tel. 237033.

Iberia, Calle 1, Avenidas 2/4, tel. 213311.

KLM, Calle 1, Avenida Central, tel. 213081.

Mexicana, Calle 1, Avenidas 2/4, tel. 221711.

Air taxi service to Tortuguero and other places not served by SANSA is provided by a number of companies listed in the phone book under "Taxis Aéreos."

Automobile Rental

Most companies charge about $20 per day and 30 cents per mile; or $40 with unlimited mileage, for a subcompact. Once you include tax, insurance and gasoline, you'll pay close to $70 per day at the unlimited mileage rate for 200 miles of driving. To check exact rates and make reservations, call the toll-free telephone numbers for the major companies in the United States and Canada. Among car-rental companies operating in San José are:

ADA Rent-A-Car, Holiday Inn, tel. 336957.

Budget, Paseo Colón, Calle 30, tel. 233284; airport, tel. 414444.

Dollar, Calle Central, Avenida 9, tel. 333339; airport, tel. 410630.

Hertz, Calle 38, Avenidas Central /1, and airport, tel. 235959.

There are others listed in the phone book under "Alquiler de Automóviles," but none offer bargains. Costs of importing and maintaining cars in Costa Rica are quite high, which is reflected in the rates.

Banks
You'll have no trouble finding a bank in downtown San José. Most are open from 9 a.m. to 3 p.m., Monday through Friday. The Banco de Costa Rica branch at Calle 7 and Avenida 1 is open until 6:30 p.m., and is convenient to some of the larger hotels. In addition, travelers checks may be cashed on weekends from 9 a.m. to 1 p.m. next to the tourist office at the Plaza de la Cultura. Watch out for pickpockets.

For tales of woe about changing travelers checks, see "Money and Banking" in the chapter of practical information.

Books, Magazines, Newspapers
New books in English, at 50 to 100 percent over U. S. prices, are available at:

Universal, Avenida Central, Calles Central /1. Large stock of English and Spanish books in a department store.

Librería Lehmann, Avenida Central, Calles 1/3. Larger stock of English and Spanish books.

The Bookshop, Avenida 1, Calles 1/3. Largest selection of English books.

Other sources are:

Casey's Donuts, Calle Central, Avenidas 7/9. "I haven't sold donuts for years," says the owner. Stacks and stacks of used books from 40 cents per.

Librería Francesa/Librería Italiana, Calle 3, Avenidas 1/ Central.

The *Tico Times,* published weekly on Fridays, is the leading English-language publication in Costa Rica, and one of the best of its kind in Latin America. Articles cover events in Costa Rica and Central America, as well as local traditions, business, entertainment, and items of human interest. The ads for lodging and services will interest many visitors.

Free publications include the *Costa Rica Grapevine Tourist Guide* and *Guide* magazine, distributed at major hotels. Both are ad vehicles for hotels, restaurants, strip joints, investment schemes, massage parlors and shops, with tidbits of practical information.

For keeping up with the world, *Time, Newsweek,* the Miami *Herald* and other imported publications are available at the bookstores mentioned above and at many hotels.

Local Buses

City buses and those serving nearby suburbs provide a service roughly comparable to that in large North American cities at a fraction of the price. The fare is usually posted near the door, and on most routes is about 10 cents.

Many bus routes start at or near the Central Park. All are identified by both a number and the name of the neighborhood or suburb they serve. These are clearly posted at the stops. In addition, 20-passenger microbuses serve some of the same areas.

Buses and their stops are given for most places of interest mentioned in this chapter. For others, ask at the tourist office.

Long-Distance Buses

Buses to various points in Costa Rica are mentioned in the coverage of towns, parks and beaches in this book. Many leave from the area of the Coca-Cola market, 16 Calle, Avenidas 1/3. For buses to other points, and to re-check schedules, inquire at the tourist office.

Service to Panama and to all Central American capitals, with connections to Mexico, is provided daily by Tica Bus, Avenida 4, Calles 9/11, tel. 218954. Nicaragua and northern Panama are also served by Sirca, Avenida 2, Calles 9/11. Other buses from the Coca-Cola terminal go as far as the Nicaraguan border at Peñas Blancas.

Churches

Among the places of worship in or near San José are:

Bahai Center, Avenida 4, Calle 22, tel. 225335.

Shaare Zion Synagogue, Paseo Colón, Calles 22/24, tel. 225449.

Church of Jesus Christ of Latter-Day Saints, Avenida 8, Calles 33/35, tel. 250208.

Carmelite Convent, San Rafael Escazú, tel. 281920.

International Chapel of St. Mary, Herradura Hotel (Catholic Mass Sunday).

Anglican Church, Avenida 4, Calles 3/5.

Union Church, Moravia. Call 275596 for free transport.

International Baptist Fellowship, San Pedro, tel. 245951 or 255218.

Doctors

Emergency medical attention for visitors is available at any public hospital. The most centrally located is Hospital San Juan de Dios, Avenida Central and Calle 16, tel. 220166. For a Red Cross ambulance, call 215818.

For treatment on a non-emergency basis, try the Clínica Bíblica, a church-related organization, at Calle 1, Avenidas 14/16, tel. 236422; or the Clínica Americana, Avenida 14, Calles Central /1, tel. 221010. Both have English-speaking doctors available, and provide service 24 hours.

Plastic surgery, by the way, is a growing non-traditional earner of foreign exchange for Costa Rica. Many a foreigner flies in to have breasts, wrinkles or nose renovated at a fraction of the cost in the States or Europe. If you're interested, check the ads in *Guide* magazine.

Embassies and Consulates

Most of the addresses below are for consulates. For those not listed, look in the phone book under "Embajadas y Consulados." Most are open mornings only.

Belgium, Los Yoses, tel. 250351.

Canada, Cronos Bldg, Calle 3, Avenida Central, tel. 230446.

El Salvador, Los Yoses, tel. 255887.

France, Calle 5, Avenidas 1/3 (No. 140), tel. 221149.

Guatemala, Avenida 1, Calles 24/28 (No. 2493), tel. 335283.

Honduras, Calle 1, Avenida 5, tel. 222145.

Italy, Calle 29, Avenidas 8/10, tel. 246574.

Mexico, Av. 7 1371, tel. 225485.

Netherlands, Los Yoses, tel. 340949.

Nicaragua, Barrio La California, tel. 339225.

Panama, San Pedro, tel. 253401.

Switzerland, Centro Colón, tel. 214829.

United Kingdom, Paseo Colón, Calles 38/40, tel. 215566.

U. S. A., Avenida 3, Calles Central /1, tel. 331155.

Entertainment

Admission to first-run American and other foreign films runs about $1.25 to $1.50 in San José. Most have sub-titles, so you'll be able to hear the original sound track. A few are dubbed into Spanish ("hablado en español," the ad will say). Newspapers give current attractions and sometimes the show times. Rarely, however, do they reveal the address of the theater, so look it up in the phone book, under "Cines," or ask at your hotel desk.

Check the billboard at the National Theater for concerts, plays and recitals, some featuring internationally known artists. Tickets are bargain-priced at 60 cents to $5. San José has a number of active theater groups, and their performances, including some open-air theater, are advertised in the newspapers.

On the raunchy side, supposedly staid San José has more than its share of strip joints. Most are located in the vicinity of Calle 2 and Avenida 8. Weak drinks are $3 to $4, the events last all night, and you ought to watch your pockets. Consult the ads in the *Grapevine Tourist Guide.*

Non-striptease musical acts are featured at the bars and night clubs of some hotels, including the Balmoral and Irazú.

Gambling

The only gaming game in town is black jack. You can play at the Club Colonial, Avenida 1, Calles 9/11; the Hotel Balmoral, Calle 7, Avenida Central; and the Hotel Irazú, on the western outskirts.

In the provinces, a more popular game is bingo, and you may want to join in if you spend some time in any small town.

The biggest game, the earner of imagined millions and a lifetime of ease for every Costa Rican, is the national lottery. By all means buy a ticket or a fraction of a ticket from a street vendor. You have a good chance of at least getting your money back if the last digit of your number is the same as that of the winner.

Libraries

For books in English, visit the library at the Centro Cultural Costarricense Norteamericano (U. S.-Costa Rican Cultural Center), in suburban San José. Call 259433 for current hours and directions. To borrow books, you'll have to become a paying member.

The other main libraries, in case you're doing serious research, are the University of Costa Rica library in San Pedro, and the National Library, Avenida 3 and Calle 15.

Maps

Detailed topographical maps, of interest to hikers, are available at the National Geographic Institute of the Ministry of Public Works, Avenida 20, Calles 9/11. Hours are 8:30 a.m. to 3:30 p.m. Assorted geographic publications are also sold, in the mornings only. Take the Barrio La Cruz bus from the Central Park to the ministry, go through the gate, turn left, and look for the "Mapas" sign.

Less detailed maps of San José and Costa Rica are distributed by the tourist office at the Plaza de la Cultura. The national map is not entirely accurate, but is serviceable for most purposes.

National Parks

The National Park Service (Servicio de Parques Nacionales) is headquartered at Calle 17, Avenida 9. Take the San Pedro bus from the Central Park. A booklet on the parks in English, with descriptions and travel advice, is sold for $1, and information is available about seasonal conditions in the more remote parks. Some of the personnel speak English. Printed material on the parks is also available at the zoo in Bolívar Park.

Pools

There are several public pools in the city, including one at La Sabana Park. The most fun, however, is Ojo de Agua, mentioned in the coverage of nearby towns, below.

Post Office

The main post office (Correos y Telégrafos, or Cortel) is at Avenida 1, Calle 2. A rate sheet is available at the counter to the left, inside the main entrance on Calle 2. General-delivery mail (lista de correos) is kept in the same place. Weigh your letters and buy stamps at the windows to the rear. The philatelic department is through a separate door, to the left of the main entrance.

Shopping

A good area for shopping is the vicinity of Calle 7 and Avenida Central. At the Centro de Artesanías Bribri, Calle 7, Avenidas Central /2, items of Indian manufacture are on sale, including woodcarvings, painted woodware, leather bags, and model ox-carts. Finer leather work, including purses, belts and shoes, is sold at Calzado La Renacente, Calle 7 and Avenida Central, while Indian weaving is sold at the National Museum. Galería Precolombina, Calle 7, Avenida Central /2, in back of the shoe store, has an assortment of genuine pre-Columbian items, from simple clay pots that go for a couple of dollars to pricey animal-form pottery. Around the corner, La Casa del Indio, Avenida 2, Calles 5/7, sells reproductions of pre-Columbian whistle pottery, leather, and silver ornaments, all at reasonable prices. Antiques will also be found in the Central Market area, and at some hotels.

The National Handicrafts Market (Mercado Nacional de Artesanías), Avenida 2 B, Calles 9/11, has a large assortment of macramé, woodcarving and the like.

The largest collection I've seen of wood, dolls, leather, t-shirts, embroidered blouses, ashtrays, pots, straw hats, jewelry, and other items ranging from silly to superb is in the gallery of stalls on Calle Central, just north of Avenida Central, on the east side of the street. Some of the leather is quite nice, and there are many items from Panama and Guatemala.

For other suggestions, see "Shopping" in the practical-information chapter of this book.

Taxis

Taxis are a surprisingly economical way for visitors to get around San José. Most trips around the city will cost less than two dollars. Fares are fixed by the government, currently at 70 cents (45 colones) for the first kilometer, 25 cents (15 colones) for each additional kilometer, and $3.00 (200 colones) per hour of waiting. These rates apply throughout the country.

Unfortunately, taxis are not metered (though the government is trying to get meters installed), and many drivers will try to cheat visitors. Calculate the distance of your trip beforehand, and settle the price with the driver before you get in. Some overpayment is inevitable. Your hotel may be able to give you some guidelines on the proper fares. Taxi drivers are not tipped.

Taxis are identified by roof lights, and are easily spotted. You may flag one down on the streets, or have one called to your hotel.

Telegrams

Radiográfica Costarricense handles domestic and international telegrams. If you have access to a private phone, you may send your telegram by dialing 123. Otherwise, take your message to the telegraph office at Avenida 5, Calle 1, or send it through your hotel operator.

Telephones

Public coin telephones are plentiful in San José, but they are not always kept in good repair, nor are the appropriate coins— 2, 5 and 10 colones — always in plentiful supply. Many stores and hotels will allow you to use their phones for a charge of 10 to 20 cents (U.S.) for a local call.

Any telephone in Costa Rica may be dialed direct from San José, without using an area code. Have plenty of coins ready for a long-distance call from a public phone.

Service and emergency numbers are as follows:

110 Collect calls within Costa Rica and operator assistance

112 Time of day

113 Telephone number information

116 International long distance (Operators speak English)

117 San José police

118 Fire department (bomberos)

127 Rural police

Tourist Office

The visitors' information center of the Instituto Costarricense de Turismo (Costa Rican Tourist Board) is located at Avenida Central and Calle 5, at the entry to the underground exhibit area in the Plaza de la Cultura. Maps, hotel brochures and a sheet of bus and train schedules are available, and extensive and up-to-date files are maintained on special-interest areas—cultural attractions, camping, and business services, to name a few. The personnel will usually try hard to obtain information they don't have. All speak English. For information by telephone, call 221090 or 216127.

Trains

The Atlantic Station of the Ferrocarril de Costa Rica (Costa Rican Railroad) is at Avenida 3, Calle 21, a few blocks east of National Park. Departure for Limón is currently at noon, and the trip takes from five to six hours. For a shorter ride on the choo-choo train, there are departures for Cartago at 4:45 p.m. and Heredia at 5:45 p.m., or you can take the Limón train as far as Cartago. To check schedules, phone 260011, extension 259. Whether or not you take the train, stop to admire the impressive steam engine of the Northern Railway (as the line was called before nationalization) on a spur in front of the station. The station is a national monument, more for historical than architectural reasons.

Trains for Puntarenas leave from the station of the Ferrocarril Eléctrico al Pacífico (Pacific Electric Railroad), Avenida 20, Calle 2, at 6:30 a.m., 10 a.m. and 3 p.m., and take about three-and-a-half hours. The Paso Ancho bus from the Central Park passes the station.

Fares on both lines are low. It costs less than $3 to go to

Limón, and proportionately less to intermediate points.

Water

Tap water in San José (and in most larger towns of Costa Rica as well) is safe to drink. But if you're wary of it, for reasons of taste or chemical difference from what you're accustomed to, or are just plain cautious, stick to bottled soda water (agua mineral).

Water pressure in much of San José is quite low. The better hotels have pressure tanks and pumps, but in more modest accommodations, you may get no more than a dribble from the tap.

Walking

Being a pedestrian in San José is at times a risky business. At some intersections, traffic lights are arranged so that it is technically impossible to cross in the clear. And even where the signals appear to be with you, many a driver will slip into gear and bear down on you the moment the light changes. Be cautious and fleet of foot.

Weather

The average daily high for San José varies hardly at all from month to month—it's almost always in the mid-seventies Fahrenheit (22 to 25 degrees Centigrade). Average nighttime lows are about 60 (15 degrees Centigrade), excellent for sleeping. Even the recorded extremes are moderate—92 is the highest temperature ever recorded in San José, 49 the lowest (33 and 9 degrees Centigrade). Precipitation, however, is quite variable. It rains almost every day from May to October (Costa Rica's "winter"), with monthly totals of about 10 inches, and the air gets to be uncomfortably sticky toward the middle of the day. The rains slacken off in November, and from January until the end of April, precipitation is a freakish event. Aside from rain, there are a number of seasonal signs in lieu of sharp differences in temperature: variations in length and clarity of daylight; the flowering of poinsettia, erythrina trees, coffee plants and other species throughout the year; and alterations in the richness of the green of surrounding hillsides.

ONE-DAY TRIPS FROM SAN JOSE

Costa Rica is small enough, and travel facilities are well enough developed, that you can reach many far points of the country by public transportation and return to your hotel in San José by nightfall. In order to actually *see* anything, however, you'll probably want to confine your one-day trips to the environs of San José and the Central Valley, e.g., Ojo de Agua springs, Poás and Irazú volcanoes, Cartago and the Orosí valley, and Alajuela and towns on the way to Sarchí. These places, and details on how to reach them, are described in the pages immediately following this section.

By taking a tour or renting a car, you can extend your one-day travel range to the Pacific beaches near Puntarenas and at Jacó, and, perhaps, the port of Limón on the Atlantic. By chartered plane, you can also make a one-day trip out of a visit to the Tortuguero reserve on the Caribbean. Day outings are also arranged through travel agencies for white-water rafting, jungle exploration, cruises in the Gulf of Nicoya, and horseback riding.

Where to go first? At the risk of sounding philistine, I will state that much of the scenery near San José is essentially similar. You'll want to be selective, especially if you're on a short trip, or wish to get down to the hard work of sunning yourself on a beach or golfing or fishing. Choose one volcano and one scenic circuit for starters, then see the other sights as time and inclination allow. Listed below are some nearby destinations in approximate order of interest.

Poás Volcano. Impressive cloud forest, craters and views, well-conceived visitors' center and exhibits.

Orosí Valley. Plunge into a broad, magnificent valley full of lush coffee farms, with colonial churches, lakes, and a river of rapids; stop at an unusual botanical garden on the way.

Aserrí or San Antonio de Escazú. Short excursions by city bus, miniature versions of the Orosí circuit.

Alajuela. Most pleasant of the nearby provincial capitals, on the way to Poás volcano. Excursion may be extended by meandering along the old road to Grecia, the furniture-making town of Sarchí, and Naranjo.

Irazú Volcano. Views as fine as those from Poás (if you hit a clear morning), but barer at the top, with few facilities.

Ojo de Agua. Fine for swimming and boating. You'll be interested if your hotel in San José has no pool.

Cartago. For those with reasons of religion.

Heredia. Stop if you have the time, while on the way to somewhere else.

Santiago Puriscal. A scenic, mountainside-clinging ride.

Visit other towns, ascend to Braulio Carrillo National Park, or go horseback riding, rafting, or boating, according to your fancy and funds, before you head to the edges of Costa Rica. For travel details, read the coverage for each of these places.

Tours and Travel Agencies

Your own style, money supply and your destination will determine whether you use a travel agent or group tours while in Costa Rica. Even if you're used to making your own way by bus and train, you'll find that only a tour, taxi or rented car will get you to the top of a volcano on certain days of the week, or all the way through the Orosí Valley without having to backtrack or trudge part of the way.

Major travel agencies are:

TAM, Calle 1, Avenidas Central /1, tel. 330044. American Express representative.

Panorama Tours, Calle 9, Avenida Central, tel. 224384.

Blanco Travel Service, Avenida Central, Calles 7/9, tel 221792.

Excai Tours (Gray Line), Avenida Central, Calles 26/28, tel. 230155.

Fiesta Tours, Avenida 1, Calles 5/7, tel. 233433.

Costa Rica Expeditions, Calle Central, Avenida 3 (P. O. Box 6941) tel. 239975. Outdoors programs (rafting, national parks, etc.). Other outdoor specialists are Horizontes, Av. 1, Calles 1/3, tel. 222022; and Ríos Tropicales, P. O. Box 472-1200, Pavas, tel. 316296.

Swiss Travel Service, Hotel Irazú, tel. 325362.

Prices and offerings vary little from agency to agency, so you'll probably book where it's most convenient. Among the usual tour offerings:

San José city tour, $12 to $16, three hours.

Irazú volcano and Cartago, $20 to $25, half day.

Lankester Gardens and Orosí valley, $12 to $16, half day.

Orosí Valley and Irazú volcano, $30 to $36, full day.

Poás volcano, $20 to $25, half day.

Heredia, Alajuela and Sarchí, $12 to $16, half day.

San José by night, $10 to $15. Even the agencies downplay this one.

Ojo de Agua, $12; Train ride to Puntarenas, $26. The most timid of travelers can do these on their own.

Train ride to Limón and return by air, $60 to $70.

Bus to Puntarenas and boat cruise in the Gulf of Nicoya, $55.

Trips to beach resorts, $100 per day.

Rafting on the Reventazón River, $65; birding, climbing and rougher rafting excursions (Costa Rica Expeditions).

Horseback rides at a farm outside San José.

Jungle tours by train or bus to Limón, then by canal launch to Tortuguero reserve and Colorado, return by air, two days, $200.

Monteverde reserve, two nights, $180.

NEARBY TOWNS

San José is surrounded by dozens of settlements, ranging from suburbs where life is a virtual extension of the urban bustle, to bucolic hillside villages where events unfold at the pace of an oxcart, within full view of the city below. You can drive from point to point in the vicinity of San José, if you have a car available. But my preference is to hop on one of the frequent suburban buses, and to look ahead and to both sides of the road, catching glimpses of local sights and goings-on, and longer views whenever the bus stops to pick up or discharge passengers. Self-made bus tours to towns near San José literally cost pennies.

MORAVIA AND CORONADO

Moravia is a handicraft center seven kilometers northeast of downtown San José. The best-known shop is the Caballo Blanco, located on one corner of the main square, where thick leather belts and furniture and a few more finely manufactured items of luggage are on display. There are various other souvenir and wicker furniture shops and stands on the road into town. The crafts alone are not enough to draw a visitor to Moravia. One also comes here to sit on the large square and watch a slower, smaller-town life than that of San José. You'll note far fewer cars on the streets than in the capital, knots of people in conversation, and an indescribable something that turns out on closer examination to be an unaccustomed quiet.

The bus for Moravia leaves from Avenida 3, Calles 1/3, San José. Get off at the stop in Moravia where most other passengers debark. This is two blocks from the square. To continue your tour, walk back to the bus stop and wait for a bus marked Coronado.

Beyond Moravia, the Coronado road rises through an area of lower-middle-class suburbs, where small and well-cared-for wood- and concrete-block homes stand in clusters among coffee groves and pasture. About one kilometer before Coronado, in Dulce Nombre, is the Instituto Clodomiro Picado of the University of Costa Rica, where snakes are studied. Ask the bus driver to let you off nearby if you wish to visit. A few rattlers, fer de lance and coral snakes are on display. Hours are 8 a.m. to 4 p.m., Monday through Friday.

After a visit to the Institute, walk or drive up the hill to Coronado, a sleepy, pleasant farming center with a surprisingly large and impressive Gothic church. Some points in town offer good views to San José, and the direct road back to the capital is lined with substantial houses that take advantage of the vistas.

Direct buses for Coronado leave from Calle 3, Avenidas 7/9, San José. You can walk down to Moravia in less than an hour, and be rewarded with sights more interesting than those in the two towns themselves.

Beyond Coronado is one of the entry points for Braulio Carrillo National Park, described later.

ASERRI

The ride out to the village of Aserrí takes the visitor through the working-class suburbs of Desamparados and San Rafael, then out into the crowded countryside, up and up over rolling hills, by rushing streams, and past farmhouse after small neat wooden or stuccoed farmhouse, each just in from the roadside, with front yard decorated with bougainvillea, hibiscus, and poinsettia. Tiny pastures and vegetable plots pass by, islands in a sea of shiny-leafed coffee trees shaded by banana plants.

Once in Aserrí, gaze down at San José, at the bottom of the teacup valley; take a look at the whitewashed, colonial-style church; and examine the Aserrí craft specialty, dolls of a rather simple sort. Catch the bus back down, or walk part of the way.

The hill town of Aserrí is only ten kilometers from San José, and 128 meters (420 feet) higher. Buses for Aserrí leave from Calle 2, Avenidas 8/10, San José.

SANTIAGO PURISCAL

Getting there is all the fun of this longer excursion through breathtaking, rolling countryside covered with coffee and orange trees, sugarcane, banana plants, and settlement after small settlement. Some 20 kilometers out from San José, the road starts to ascend to country of pine and oak, and precipitous mountainside pastures where some force other than gravity appears to hold cattle to earth. To either side of the road are sheer drops of a thousand feet and more. Each hairpin turn frames a new view of the Central Valley, increasingly far below.

At about kilometer 30, on the crest of the southern ridge, is the Guayabo reserve of the Quitirrisi Indians. The Quitirrisi live like other rural Costa Ricans, but they are poorer, less well educated, and have a limited command of Spanish. Their horizons are largely limited to the boundaries of their settlement. You'll notice Indians alongside the road with bundles of baskets, which are woven from vines, and sold in San José.

Buses for Santiago Puriscal leave about every 45 minutes from the Coca-Cola station, Calle 16, Avenidas 1/3. The trip takes about an hour, but one can get off around the Indian reserve and walk for a while (take a sweater), then catch a return bus.

SAN ANTONIO DE ESCAZU

The hill village of San Antonio de Escazú features a fine Ravenna-style church, and good views down to San José, and across to the hump-shaped volcano Barva. Brightly painted ox-carts are in use as a practical means of moving goods in an era of expensive gasoline, and not merely to please the eye of visitors. On the way is the town of Escazú, where many foreigners make their homes. Rural, slow, clean, sunny, industrious and quite civilized, San Antonio appears to have been transplanted from hills somewhere above the Mediterranean Sea.

Buses from San Antonio leave from Calle 16, Avenidas 1/3, San José.

The Central Valley

In almost every way, the Central Valley is the heart and soul of Costa Rica. Most of the population lives on this twenty-by-fifty mile plateau, bordered to the north by the Poás, Barva, Irazú and Turrialba volcanoes, and to the south by an older mountain ridge. Almost all of Costa Rica's industry, most of the all-important coffee crop, and much produce for home consumption come from here. Public administration, education and power generation are centered in this mini-state.

And as if all the facts about industry and agriculture and human resources were not sufficient for one small region, the Central Valley is blessed as well with more than its share of natural beauty: great valleys carpeted with coffee trees, and broken by waterfalls, rippling streams, and rivers of rapids; pine groves and pastures on rolling hills; rocky canyons and lakes; a climate as benign and temperate as any on earth, where almost anything will grow; slumbering volcanoes, their slopes carved into farms of neat squares; and small, well-built houses everywhere. It is as close to one's idealized vision of the "country" as one is likely to get.

And yet, hardly a part of the Central Valley is really rural. Paved highways reach almost every point, giant electricity pylons step across the landscape, rivers are dammed and harnessed at every edge of the plateau. A cement factory, a knitting mill, rises amid pastures and coffee. Town gives way to fields and then to village and fields and town, each settlement with its dominating church and flowered gardens.

Nevertheless, man and nature appear for all the world to live in beauteous harmony. All of man's intrusions might have been placed with a sense of how things look, how they interrelate, and

73

how they are kept up. It is this machine-in-the-garden aspect of the Central Valley that is especially attractive, and unique in this part of the world.

The Central Valley is the part of Costa Rica that sometimes is called the Switzerland of Central America. In fact, there is nothing Swiss about the climate, or the tin-roofed houses. The bare statistics of per-capita income would not earn the population a place at the lowest social rung of any Swiss settlement. Only contented cows munching in mountainside pastures present a roughly comparable vista. But in the apparent industriousness of the people, in their concentration and use of all resources at hand, in their general public orderliness, it could be said that the Swiss are somewhat reminiscent of the Costa Ricans of the Central Valley.

Not that all is sublime at the heart of Costa Rica. Aside from the economic shocks of recent times, there are natural shocks. Volcanoes erupt periodically and spew ashes, boulders and destruction. Earthquakes shake down houses and cathedrals. People, too, are not always kind to the land when they live so near one to another. A close look reveals that many a gurgling stream is off-color or slimy, and lined with trash. But by the standards of the region, and of many a more developed area, most things are well.

The volcanoes of the Cordillera Central to the north are the source of the contours and the wealth of the Central Valley. Much of the land was shaped over many centuries, as volcanic ejecta and lava showered, washed down and oozed, to settle into two basins, separated by the low hills that lie between the present cities of Cartago and San José. The lava made for a natural fertility, renewed by periodic eruptions.

Pine forests dominated these basins for centuries. The Spaniards found the climate at altitudes of 900 to 1500 meters ideal for subsistence agriculture, if not for weath-producing plantation crops, and began to cut back the natural cover. Coffee trees, of course, came eventually to be the main vegetation in the valley, complemented, according to slight differences in altitude, by sugarcane, corn, and pasture. Coffee is now to Costa Rica what citrus fruit is to Israel. Yields per acre and caffeine content are among the highest in the world.

Coffee trees are what visitors will see most as they tour the

74

Central Valley, but how these are seen depends on the time of year. Always the trees are shiny-leaved, crowded, and usually pampered in the shade of larger trees. Shortly into the rainy season, they glisten with moisture. Dozens of delicate, white-fingered blossoms erupt on each branch, then shower down. For most of the growing season the berry (cereza, or cherry) is green, turning red and finally to oxblood when ready for picking.

The rains are mostly over when the armies of coffee pickers enter the dusty fields, protected by heavy shirts and leggings and rubber boots from the abrasions of dense branches. The coffee harvest is a fabled time of hard work, crucial to the well-being of the nation, and the president himself hands out awards to the best workers. Ripe berries are selected by hand, dumped from baskets to carts, and hurried to the mills where simple machines scrape off their outer hulls. The slime that coats the beans is soaked off by a day of fermenting, then the beans are spread, sun-dried during the day on concrete platforms, and mounded and covered by night. A second skin is rubbed off, the beans are sorted and polished, and a government agency supervises the orderly marketing of the crop. Harvest time is when the plantations are busiest, but throughout the year, workers plant and prune and clear and fertilize and otherwise tend the trees.

The relatively advanced development of the Central Valley makes it easy for the visitor to explore. Roads go everywhere, and on most of them, buses both comfortable and frequent. Good hotels and restaurants are not part of the valley's blessings, though there are some establishments worthy of recommendation; and no place is far from the haven of San José.

CARTAGO

Population: 31,500; Altitude: 1450 meters (4756 feet); 23 kilometers from San José.

Defeated in their attempts to found viable settlements in the merciless lowlands, the early Spanish settlers of Costa Rica turned their attention to the temperate uplands. In 1564, Juan Vásquez de Coronado, the Spanish governor, was able to write to the king:

75

Basilica of Cartago

"I have never seen a more beautiful valley, and I laid out a city between two rivers. I named the city Cartago, because this province also bears that name."

The Guarco valley, where the new head settlement was sited, had abundant water, fertile earth, and a population of a few thousand who were less hostile to Vásquez than the natives of the coast had been to his more belligerent predecessors. While the colonists did not succeed in establishing full dominion over the colony from their new highland base, nor in subjecting native peoples to labor on vast plantations of export crops, they at least were able to till subsistence crops and hold their own. In and around Cartago, which remained little more than an impoverished village for many years, was Costa Rica born and shaped.

Cartago lost its central position toward the end of the colonial period, as Costa Rica achieved a rough prosperity and settlement pushed westward in the Central Valley. The relative decline of the city was affirmed shortly after independence, when the capital was moved to San José.

Costa Rica's old capital is today not at all colonial in flavor. Virtually all structures of the pre-independence period were damaged or destroyed by a string of natural disasters: earthquakes in 1841 and 1910, and intermittent rains of ash and debris from the always-threatening volcano Irazú that looms over the city to the north.

But despite its political decline, Cartago remains the religious capital. Ten blocks east of the main square of the city is the Basílica de Nuestra Señora de Los Angeles (Basilica of Our Lady of the Angels), with its six-inch-high black statue of the Virgin, the object of special devotion on August 2, and of pilgrimages throughout the year.

According to tradition, the little statue was discovered on the outskirts of Cartago on August 2, 1635, by a girl named Juana Pereira. It was twice removed and placed in a box, and each time miraculously reappeared in its original location. Yielding to divine will so clearly expressed, the ecclesiastical authorities decided to build a church where the Virgin had been found. The statuette twice was stolen from its shrine, in 1824 and 1950, but each time was returned. The original church was damaged in the 1910 earthquake, and the present basilica dates from 1926.

That is the religious background, which is considerably more impressive than the structure itself. The basilica stands out as a conglomerate of confused styles, roughly Byzantine at the front, with a motley collection of angels grafted on, domes bubbling overhead, barren, gray stone blocks forming the sides and rear. It is as if the officials of the Church realized that they had to do something for their Virgin, but with no national artistic tradition to draw on, they found themselves at a loss as to how to go about it.

The interior of the basilica is no better. Vaults and columns painted in splotches of green and brown and glittering silver defocus one's attention from the altar. Poor taste completes itself with billboards on the basilica's lawn advertising its soda shop.

The shrine of La Negrita, as the statue is familiarly called, is below ground level. Nearby is a room full of discarded crutches, and miniature gold and silver hands, legs, arms, and assorted other parts of the body, all testifying to the healing powers of the Virgin and of the waters that flow from the spring under her shrine.

Back at the center of Cartago are the more esthetically pleasing ruins of the Church of the Convent (Iglesia del Convento, or, more simply, Las Ruinas). Only the massive, moss-encrusted, stone-block walls remain of this colonial structure, with their simple, pleasing, Moorish-Spanish contours. The roof fell in during the 1910 earthquake, after the structure had been damaged in previous tremors, and the church was abandoned. The walls now enclose a gardened space, where bougainvillea, pines and a lovely pond attract a variety of birds. The cobbled section of street in front of the church adds to the atmospherics.

Visiting Cartago

Aside from its religious structures, Cartago is on the routes to the Irazú volcano and the Orosí valley. Buses for Cartago leave from Avenida Central, Calle 13, San José, about every 20 minutes from 5 a.m. to 11 p.m.

Do not try to stay overnight in Cartago! The one decent hotel recently closed, and those that remain, all clustered a block up from the market, across the railroad tracks, are fleabag, noisy dives of the worst sort. (I know!) You'll do far better to leave San José on the 5 a.m. bus if you're planning to ascend Irazú by public bus from Cartago.

The food situation is mildly brighter in Cartago. The Salón París, on the main street opposite one corner of the market, offers main courses of simple fare for about $4, sandwiches for $1. Despite the name, the decor features Venetian and bullfight scenes. There are numerous other modest sodas and restaurants around, including, of course, the soda of the basilica.

IRAZU VOLCANO

At 3432 meters (11260 feet), Irazú is the highest volcano in Costa Rica. It is also one of the most active, and certainly the most feared, a rumbling presence of continuing steaming, boiling and fuming that has practically destroyed the city of Cartago on more than one occasion, and played continuing havoc with the lives of farmers who till the soil and raise livestock on its slopes. But paradoxically, the volcano is also a benefactor. Its ash renews the richness of the soil, even while it blocks water pipes and roads.

Irazú's most recent active cycle started with a bang on

March 13, 1963, when boulders and ash began to rain down on homes and farms near the volcano's peak. Over a two-year period, rivers in the vicinity of Cartago were dammed and the city flooded; corrosive ash fell like a gray snowstorm over San José, damaging water pumps, home furnishings, and many a respiratory system. Dairy production plummeted as pastures were seared or covered over, and output of coffee and vegetables likewise fell. With help from abroad, dikes were hurriedly constructed to divert deviant waters from doing further damage, and the millions of tons of ash were swept up and carted away. Irazú's peak assumed a new form as part of the mountain collapsed into the space vacated by magma. Even today, spurts of sulphurous smoke, steam and water are part of a continuing reformation and growth of the mountain.

The distinction of Irazú among volcanoes in the modern world is that it is one of the few semi-active ones that can easily be viewed up close. A paved highway climbs right to the peak, which is protected as a national park. If you happen to ascend when the peak is free of clouds—a near impossibility during the rainy season, and an uncertain condition even in dry times—you'll be rewarded with views to both oceans, or at least to a good part of the country.

The ride up Irazú proceeds slowly, through pastures and corn fields. Past the town of Cot, the air becomes increasingly windy and cold, and the trees more twisted. On the cool, ash-fertilized slopes, potatoes are the main crop, along with carrots and onions. And there are many dairy farms, all now recovered from the 1963-65 calamities, and awaiting the next ones.

Sites on the way up Irazú include the neat farming villages of Potrero Cerrado and Tierra Blanca, each dominated by a church; a pair of *miradores*, or lookout points, furnished with concrete picnic stools; and a rambling, white, tile-roofed sanatorium that takes advantage of the mountain air. About 20 kilometers out of Cartago, and 12 kilometers from the crater, is the Hotel de Montaña Irazú, where a night in cool, rustic comfort costs about $10 per person.

Over the last few kilometers of the ascent, the face of the mountain changes dramatically, from green pasture to oak forest laden with epiphytes at the park boundary, then to a seared, boulder-strewn primeval surface of ash and bare soil where wind-beaten ferns and shrubs maintain a tenuous hold. Around the next turn, one half expects to encounter a herd of dinosaurs poking their heads through the mist. Charred tree trunks stand as monuments to the last period of intense activity, while a few younger saplings take root for what will probably be an abbreviated life in the severe surroundings.

Once atop Irazú, you can examine a small exhibit on geysers, fumaroles, mudpots, ash, and other forms and evidence of volcanic activity. Slog through the ash and view the craters—slowly. The air at this altitude is short of oxygen, and you will be short of breath, as well as buffeted by wind and mist. The Diego de la Haya crater contains a lake, tinted to a rusty hue by dissolved minerals. The main, western crater, which swallowed up several earlier craters, currently shows virtually no activity or gas emissions. There are active fumaroles on the northwestern slope. Much of this, it bears emphazing, will not be visible because of the clouds that shroud the peak even during much of the dry season. But even when the top of Irazú is clouded over, a few minutes of exposure to the nasty environment and a glimpse of the fantasy-world landscape will be long remembered.

Visitors to Irazú should be prepared with warm clothing. A couple of sweaters will do, though a down ski jacket would not be too much. Raingear will help during the rainy season and even during the rest of the year, when wind-borne moisture will sting the skin.

Buses for the peak of Irazú leave on Mondays, Thursdays, Saturdays and Sundays from in front of the bus terminal in Cartago, next to the market and a block uphill from the main square. Departure times are 6:30 a.m. and 1:30 p.m., but these hours are approximate, so it would be best to show up at 6 a.m. (or 1 p.m., at more risk of cloud cover). The bus may be marked "Cot" or "Tierra Blanca," (towns on the volcano's slopes), as well as "Irazú." Fare is about $1. The ride up takes an hour and a half, a half-hour is allowed at the crater (it really is enough for most visitors), and the descent takes another half hour. If you want to walk part way, other buses go as far as Tierra Blanca, about halfway up from Cartago. The crater is 32 kilometers from Cartago, or 54 kilometers from San José. If you're driving, you'll find the route well marked. There's a nominal admission charge to the volcano, usually collected only at busy times.

The Orosí Valley

East of Cartago is the well-traveled scenic circuit through the Orosí Valley. The route covers only about 55 kilometers from Cartago, easily driven at a leisurely pace in a couple of hours. Bus travel of the whole route requires some backtracking, but a trip to the halfway point will give you more than half the available pleasure.

About seven kilometers east of Cartago is the Lankester Botanical Garden (Jardín Lankester) of the University of Costa Rica. If you're driving, you'll see the Ricalit roofing factory on the left just before the side road to the gardens on the right. By public transportation, take the Paraíso bus from the Cartago terminal to the Ricalit factory, then walk one-half kilometer down the side road to the south, to the entrance.

The Lankester Garden is most famed for its orchid collection, the largest of its kind in the world. But there is much, much more in this well-planned wonderland: bromeliads and other epiphytes, acres and acres of transplanted hardwoods, fruit trees, bamboo groves, cacti, medicinal aloe plants, dreamy and deadly nightshade, and many others. Species are identified only by Latin tags, but you'll recognize some as houseplants, especially in the more jungly areas, where ponds are crossed with the aid of bridges made from vines. One large section has been left untended to grow back into native forest.

The garden is open from 9 a.m. to noon and 1 to 3 p.m. every day, with guided walks on the hour. You can wander through at other times, but you'll be assigned an employee as a tail to make sure that you stick to the brick path and don't pick anything. Admission is about $1.

To continue your trip without a car, go back to the highway and pick up a bus marked "Orosí."

A couple of kilometers past Paraíso on the road to the south is a mirador, or lookout point. Take advantage of it if you can for 20-mile views down into the great Orosí valley, carpeted with pasture and, of course, coffee forest. The Río Grande de Orosí snakes along at the bottom and joins the Río Macho to form the Río Reventazón—the Foaming River. The town of Orosí and smaller clusters of houses and ranches can be picked out as clearly as if you were flying overhead. This is surely one of the most spectacular views in a country of spectacular views, superior in clarity to any road map.

After the lookout point, the road twists and descends into the valley, and finally straightens and runs flat along the Reventazón River, through coffee groves to the garden town of Orosí. Here is a lovely restored colonial church dating from the mid-eighteenth century, with brightly whitewashed walls and red tile roof. The church houses a small collection of religious art. There are hot springs on the edge of town, and swimming pools a kilometer down the road, but you can safely save your swimming for later. Farther on are the Río Macho electric works, along a branch road.

Past the bridge two kilometers from Orosí is Palomo, known mainly for the Motel Río, which is right at the end of the bridge, without an identifying sign. The motel has a number of cabins and an oversized swimming pool (there's a small charge to use it), overlooking the rushing Reventazón. The restaurant is best known for its river fish and also serves steaks. Main courses cost about $5, and the cane-ceilinged pavilion dining area is pleasant. You can phone the motel at 519191 to reserve for a night in the country. The rate is about $15 double, and well worth it.

The bus for Orosí ends its run near the Motel Río. Without a car, you can walk or hitch a ride toward the Cachí dam, or backtrack to Cartago to pick up a bus to Cachí, through Ujarrás.

Continuing by car (or tour bus), you'll proceed about eight kilometers to the Cachí Dam, one of the larger hydroelectric projects of the Central Valley. Turning back and heading to the north, you'll then come to Ujarrás, and a Spanish mission, one of the first churches in colonial Costa Rica. According to tradition, a humble Huetar Indian fished a box from a river and carried it to Ujarrás, from where it could not be budged. When opened, it was found to contain an image of the Virgin. A church was built on the site, in about 1560. A few years later, when the British pirates Mansfield and Morgan landed at Portete, a force was hastily organized to expel the invaders. After a prayer stop at Ujarrás, the defenders marched to the Caribbean, where they defeated the superior English force. The victory was attributed to the Virgin of Ujarrás. The church was later abandoned after a series of earthquakes and floods, and the image, now less recalcitrant, was taken to Paraíso. But the ruins remain a pleasing sight. They are the locale of an annual tribute to the Virgin.

The last stopping point on the Orosí circuit is the Ujarrás lookout point, high above the valley, where the highway starts to curve back to the west, toward Paraíso and Cartago. Take a good look before you leave the scenery behind.

TURRIALBA

Population: 25,500; altitude: 625 meters (2050 feet); 64 kilometers from San José.

Located where the Central Valley starts to slope down toward the Atlantic jungles, Turrialba is lower, warmer, more languid, and less tidy than the towns nearer to San José. Turrialba marks the approximate limit of coffee cultivation. The valley of the Reventazón in this area typically is pastured or planted in sugarcane along its lower, flatter reaches, and covered with coffee trees on its upper slopes.

Most visitors will not bother to get off the train or bus at Turrialba, which is basically an agricultural center of no great attraction. But those with a special interest in agriculture or archaeology may want to make a stop.

A few kilometers east of town is CATIE, the Tropical Agronomic Research and Education Center, where an international team of scientists studies and promotes methods to increase the productivity of agriculture in the warmer regions. The varied altitudes near the institute afford a variety of environments for testing plant and animal strains, and more efficient ways of cultivating traditional crops. There is a large, specialized library. Visitors are welcome at the institute, which is about a $2 taxi ride from town. Guided tours may be arranged in advance by phoning 566431, or through travel agencies in San José.

About 20 kilometers north of Turrialba, on the slopes of the Turrialba volcano, is the Guayabo National Monument. Although Costa Rica is especially rich in pre-Columbian antiquities, its early inhabitants lived nomadic existences, or concentrated in villages and towns built of highly perishable materials. There are no great native ceremonial centers that survive to this day, as they do in Honduras, Guatemala, El Salvador, and Mexico, or at least they have not yet been discovered. Which is why the

Guayabo complex, with its constructions of natural and hewn stone, is considered important by Costa Ricans, although it is unsophisticated and relatively modest in extent.

The Guayabo site includes paved walkways, walls and circular stone constructions that might have been foundations for houses of a South American sort. Subterranean and surface aqueducts, also signs of South American cultural influence, are still serviceable. Other finds are fluted points, scrapers and knives which show stylistic influences from both north and south; and carved stone tables, grave markers and blocks of undetermined purpose, which might have been altars. Some of the markings on the stone objects are obviously persons or gods, but most are non-representational, and remain a mystery to modern viewers.

Archeologists estimate that Guayabo was occupied by 800 A.D. and abandoned, for undetermined reasons, from 100 to 200 years before the Spanish first came to Costa Rica. In the absence of historical records, the goings-on at the site remain a mystery, though it appears that Guayabo was some sort of center for a number of nearby villages. Since it was situated on a natural route from the highlands to the Atlantic, it may also have been a trading center.

Aside from the ruins, Guayabo is a good birding area, and contains a small section of undisturbed premontane rain forest. Camping is permitted at the site.

Access to Guayabo National Monument from Turrialba is by an unpaved road in poor condition. Buses for Guayabo currently leave the Turrialba bus station Monday at 3 p.m., Wednesday at 11:30 a.m. and Friday at 1:30 p.m., with irregular return times. Buses for Santa Teresita, five kilometers from Guayabo, leave Turrialba daily at 11 a.m. and 6:30 p.m.

Farther north of Turrialba is the semi-active volcano of the same name, which rises to an altitude of 3339 meters (10955 feet). Access for climbing the volcano is usually from the village of Santa Cruz, north of the town of Turrialba, or from the picturesque town of Pacayas, which may be reached by bus from San José or Cartago.

One last, adventurous excursion from Turrialba is to Moravia de Chirripó, 30 kilometers away in the mountains to the east. In the region are small settlements of Talamanca Indians, who after centuries of isolation are coming into contact with the main-

84

stream culture of Costa Rica. Inquire in Turrialba for buses or trucks headed to Moravia.

Buses for Turrialba leave from Avenida Central, Calle 13, San José, about every half hour from 5 a.m. to 9 p.m. The trip takes less than two hours. You may also take the train from San José (currently at noon) or from Limón (6 a.m.), or a bus from Limon. Very modest accommodations are available at the Central, Chamanga and Interamericano hotels. The latter has a few rooms with private bath.

HEREDIA

Population: 33,000; Altitude: 1152 meters (3779 feet); 11 kilometers from San José.

Founded in 1706 at the foot of the extinct Barva volcano by migrants from Cartago, Heredia is a short commute from San José. The Atirro coffee mill, one of Costa Rica's largest, is on the outskirts; the National University is located here; and there are some impressive mansions on the western side of town. But most of the population is working-class, and the central area has a down-at-the-heels air.

Nevertheless, there are some architectural gems in Heredia. The main church on the central park, dating from 1797, is one of the few in Costa Rica that survive from the colonial period. With massive walls of stuccoed stone blocks stained brown and black and overgrown with moss, a triangular pediment, and an almost separate, squat bell tower, it is a near-perfect example of the public architectural style of the last years of Spanish rule. The low contours were meant to resist earthquakes, or at least control damage from vibrating, toppling towers and walls. The church is also one of the more atmospheric buildings in Costa Rica, without excessive restoration and sprucing up.

Set back from the north side of the park is El Fortín, the old Spanish fortress tower that is the symbol of Heredia. With gun slits that widen to the exterior, in defiance of standard military architecture, El Fortín stands as an unintended symbol of Costa Rica's non-belligerent nature. A number of other buildings on the square have a colonial air, with colonnades and aging tile

85

roofs.

One last item to see in Heredia is an art deco church on the secondary square at Calle 6 and Avenida 8. It's homely, but cute in its way.

While Heredia's attractions are not to everybody's taste, the town is on the way to Alajuela and the Barva and Poás volcanoes. Do stop by if you have the time. Buses for Heredia leave from Calle 8, Avenidas Central /1, microbuses from Calle 1, Avenidas 5/7, San José. Bus service is also available from the Alajuela terminal.

North of Heredia, on the slopes of Barva, is the village of San José de la Montaña, 20 kilometers from San José, where a couple of hotels take advantage of the broad views and fresh mountain air. The best is the Hotel de Montaña El Pórtico, just northwest of town, with 12 rooms, a restaurant, sauna and pool. Rates are $17 single, $23 double. Telephone 376022, or 212039 in San José to arrange transportation. (Mailing address: Apartado 289, San José.) Farther on are the Cabañas de Montaña Cypresal, where units have kitchenettes, and horseback riding is available, as well as a swimming pool and sauna. Rates are about $20 double. Phone 374466, or write to Apartado 7891, San José. Either of these places would make a fine base for touring San José and the Central Valley, if you decide to rent a car. Buses run from Heredia to San José de la Montaña, but not all the way to the hotels.

Farther north from Heredia is Braulio Carrillo National Park, which takes in the extinct Barva and Cacho Negro volcanoes. The park was established to protect the flora and fauna along a new highway to Guápiles, in the Caribbean region. Though off the beaten track at the moment, the park will probably become quite frequented as the road comes into use. The new highway will roughly follow a historic cart road that connected San José with the railhead at Carrillo, before the line from Limón to San José was completed.

Carrillo Park, which varies in altitude from 500 meters to 2906 meters (9534 feet, the peak of Barva volcano), encompasses tropical wet forest, premontane wet forest, and montane wet forest, or cloud forest. All that "wet" means that branches are laden with orchids, bromeliads and mosses, while ferns, shrubs and much else compete with trees for floor space. On the Atlantic slope are numerous waterfalls and pools that evidence the great year-round rainfall. Strong winds blow through, between the Irazú and Barva volcanoes.

Common animals in Carrillo Park include foxes, coyotes, white-faced, spider and howler monkeys, ocelots, sloths, and several species of poisonous snakes. More than 500 bird species have been catalogued, including the uncommon quetzal, the long-tailed symbol of liberty whose feathers were treasured in ancient Mesoamerica. Spottings of the quetzal are usually made in the forest atop Barva.

Facilities in Carrillo Park are currently in a state of development, and it would be a good idea to check with the park service in San José before planning a visit. There are two entrances. One is 20 kilometers from Heredia, reached via a road through San José de la Montaña and the horse country and oak forest beyond. This route is often muddy, and is passable for certain only in the dry season. By public transportation, take a Paso Llano bus from Heredia, get off at the Sacramento crossroads, and start hiking. It's about three hours to the crater lake atop Barva.

The Alto de la Palma entrance, along the new highway, is 20 kilometers north of Moravia. Follow the signs for Bajo de la Hondura if you're driving. Otherwise take a bus to San Jerónimo from Avenida 5, Calle 3, San José, and hike about 10 kilometers onward to the park entry.

From Heredia, a highway climbs north past the turnoff for the Poás volcano (described later), then plunges down to the plains of San Carlos, ending at Puerto Viejo on the Sarapiquí River, 70 kilometers distant. Along the way are the dramatic La Paz falls, located at Vara Blanca, just after the Poás turnoff. Farther north, a branch road at San Miguel leads to Venecia de San Carlos. About five kilometers to the north of Venecia are the ruins of Cutris, a pre-Columbian city that shows signs of having been well ordered, with wide streets. The road from Venecia comes to within two kilometers of the site, which has not been restored and has no visitors' facilities.

The San Carlos plain, despite its proximity to the Central

Valley, is a frontier area, where a waterlogged terrain and assorted pests and illnesses until recently obstructed settlement. Even now, hardly a road penetrates the area, and rivers are the main transport routes. More and more people have moved to the San Carlos plain in recent years from the crowded central part of Costa Rica, to raise cattle and subsistence crops. The San Juan River forms the northern border of the region with Nicaragua, but it is hardly a barrier. People and goods circulate freely and without formality between the two countries along the many waterways, much to the consternation of political authorities. And in troubled recent times, some of the movement has been far from innocent.

Light cargo boats operate on the Sarapiquí and San Juan Rivers between Puerto Viejo and Barra del Colorado, at the northern end of the Tortuguero Canal. You may be able to negotiate your way aboard one, and thus make a round trip back to San José via the Tortuguero reserve and Limón, or by flying back from Colorado. Patience and a flexible schedule are absolute requirements for the journey, as floods and fancy will play havoc with promised departures. Only the most basic of accommodations are available at Puerto Viejo. There are usually several buses a day to Puerto Viejo from San José. Even if you're not planning to go onward from Puerto Viejo, a bus ride out this way is an interesting and scenic excursion to an end-of-the-road point seen by few outsiders.

ALAJUELA

Population: 47,700; Altitude: 941 meters (3087 feet); 23 kilometers from San José.

Located just a short ride west of the capital, Alajuela is Costa Rica's second city, founded late in the colonial period, in 1790. Bustling, with a climate warmer than San José's, Alajuela is an important cattle marketing and sugar-processing center, and, increasingly, a site for small manufacturing industries. The denizens of the town are famously good humored, and well they might be, for Alajuela is the most pleasant of the provincial capitals, a place where lingering around the square is the chief diversion, and a recommendable one.

Alajuela's main claim to fame is as the birthplace of Juan Santamaría, the drummer boy who set fire to the headquarters of the American adventurer William Walker in 1857, thus helping to bring about the defeat of the filibuster forces that had taken control of Nicaragua. A statue of the Erizo (the "Hedgehog," as Santamaría is affectionately known, for his bristly hair,) may be seen a block south of the main square, on Calle 2. Torch in hand, rifle at his side, he stands ready to repeat his deed.

The main square of Alajuela is a shady forest-garden, with mango and palm trees, where locals and not a small number of resident foreigners observe the passing of the day from stone benches. Also hanging out in the park, more literally, are a few two-toed sloths, those snail-slow creatures that look slug-ugly in photos but are cute and furry in the flesh. Assorted statuary and fountains complete the picture. Bordering the park are a number of substantial old buildings from the coffee-boom days, with massive walls, stone-trimmed windows, iron grilles, and, in one instance, corner turrets.

Facing the east side of the central park is the city's main church, an uninteresting neo-classical structure with simple lines. (For orientation purposes, Calle Central runs along the east side of the park, by the church, Avenida Central along the south. The street numbering system is the same as in San José, though few streets are marked.)

About five blocks east of the central park is a more attractive church, built in a Costa Rican simplified baroque style, with angels popping up around the edge of the facade.

A block north of the square is the Juan Santamaría Historical Museum, housed in the solid building at the corner of Calle 2 and Avenida 3. Costa Ricans and Yanqui-bashers will examine the artifacts and battle paintings of the Walker war. Others will admire the building itself, with its wide archways, massive beams, whitewashed walls and tile roof. William Walker continues to serve a rather useful purpose in Costa Rica, as an outlet for any resentments against Americans, who are generally liked. If you get into a conversation on the subject, be sure to condemn Walker's acts of more than a hundred years ago, which were, in fact, despicable. The man sought to re-institute slavery, held elections of doubtful validity, and found excuses to break numerous promises and betray his friends.

Getting to Alajuela

The city is just a short hop from San José. It you're driving, take the Cañas highway (Autopista General Cañas, or simply "la pista") with its laughable tolls—currently less than 10 cents. Microbuses leave from Calle 14, Avenidas 1/3, San José, every 15 minutes or so, until about 10 p.m.; buses leave from Calle 12, Avenidas 3/4. The microbus terminal in Alajuela is at Avenida 4, Calles 2/4, two blocks south of the square. The Alajuela bus station is at Calle 8, Avenidas Central /1, three blocks west of the square.

Accommodations

The Hotel Alajuela, Calle 2, Avenidas Central /2, a half-block from the square, is a fairly clean, homey, and relatively modern establishment, with modest rooms. At $3 to $4 single, $5 to $6 double, it's one of the best budget hotel buys around. Rooms on the street side can be quite noisy. There are no other decent hotels in downtown Alajuela, and only a dozen rooms in this hotel, so call before you come, to make sure there's room. The number is 411241. (Hint: Alajuela is only a half-hour from San José by frequent bus and microbus.)

There are a couple of acceptable restaurants. The best is the Cencerro, upstairs on Avenida Central, facing the park. Charcoal-broiled steaks are the specialty, but there are fish and chicken dishes as well. Entrees run $4 to $5.

A block behind the Cencerro, on Avenida 2, is the Restaurant Antorcha (named for Juan Santamaría's torch, as are many other establishments of various sorts). This is a cavernous place, and also, apparently, an honorable one. A sign reads: "No se permiten escenas amorosas" ("amorous scenes prohibited"). You are warned! Simply prepared (perhaps "wholesome" is the word) meat and fish dishes for $3 to $5, sandwiches $1, organ music free on weekend evenings.

For Mexican food, try El Sarape, Calle 2 and Avenida 2, a block south from the square, and upstairs. This is a big, dark bar with recorded mariachi music. If you can't see the menu, order the combination plate (entremés surtido) for $4. Other Mexican snack items run about $2, and there are the usual Costa Rican

90

steak and chicken dishes for $4 to $5.

If you're planning to eat breakfast in Alajuela before catching the bus to Poás volcano, you'll have a problem. Restaurants on two corners of the square, the Aeropuerto and Soda La Hiedra, serve eggs that are greasy beyond digestibility. Limit yourself to a cup of coffee at either place, then buy some pastries at ItalPan, a block and a half south of the park on Avenida Central.

Once you've made the rounds of Alajuela, you'll have your choice of continuing to Poás volcano, Ojo de Agua springs, a couple of tropical zoos, and the towns of Grecia, Sarchí and Naranjo; which places are described below in that order.

POAS VOLCANO

Poás has several distinctions. It has the largest geyser-type crater in the world—1.5 kilometers across and 300 meters deep. It contains two lakes, one in an extinct crater, one in the fuming main crater. It is in continuing activity, in the form of seeping gases and steam, as well as occasional geysers and the larger eruptions of every few years (the last in 1978). Most practically for the visitor, it is easily reached by a paved road, and the facilities atop the mountain are the best in the national park system. The peak of the volcano is 2704 meters (8871 feet) above sea level.

The ascent of Poás starts at Alajuela, if you go by bus. By car, two routes are available, through Alajuela or Heredia. These converge at the little village of Poasito, high on the volcano's slopes. Either way, the visitor ascends through coffee, cattle and horse country. I won't bother to describe in detail the increasingly dramatic and grandiose vistas that are afforded of the Central Valley and of distant volcanoes and mountain ridges as the road winds onward and upward into pine and oak altitudes, since such landscapes have been mentioned elsewhere.

The climate atop Poás is less severe than that on Irazú; the peak is several hundred meters lower, and the steam and gases burn out a smaller area. Vegetation is therefore more abundant. But on a windy day, or when the peak is enshrouded in a dripping pea soup, the visitor will find nothing benign about the environment. Nighttime temperatures well below freezing are not uncommon.

Much of the upper part of Poás is cloud forest, the enchanted, cool, moist environment where orchids and bromeliads and vines thrive at every level, along with humble ferns and mosses on the ground. The Poás cloud forest is especially rich in mushrooms and lichens. Parts of the national park are former pastures that are being allowed to return to their natural states; these contain many oak trees. Other sections near the peak are meadow-like, or are characterized by low shrubs and gnarled and twisted trees.

Wildlife in the Poás forest is not abundant, possibly due to intense farming on the surrounding slopes. Among the inhabitants are brocket deer, coatis, sloths, cougars, and the Poás squirrel, which has been found only in this vicinity. Birds include several types of hummingbirds, trogons, and the emerald toucanet among more than 70 recorded species.

The substantial visitors' center includes an auditorium where a half-hour slide show about the national parks is given several times a day. The narration is in Spanish, but the scenes make the show worthwhile, even if you don't understand the words. Restaurant facilities are planned, but it would be wise to bring a snack in case these are not yet open at the time of your visit.

Orient yourself at the exhibit area before walking around, since you'll be covering a lot of territory. Aside from a model of the volcano and its craters, there are some wonderful peek-a-boo contraptions where you can try to identify animals by their tracks; samples of volcanic products; volcanic cross-sections; and descriptions of the extensive flora of Costa Rica.

From the visitors' center, you'll probably head first to the main crater. Along the walkway you'll notice the plant called the sombrilla del pobre (poor man's parasol), which is characteristic of the open areas of Poás. The leaves grow up to two meters across, which explains the name and occasional use of the plant.

Visitors are not allowed to descend into the fuming main crater, but the views from its rim are impressive. At the bottom is a lake formed by rain water, its shade of green changing according to the amount of sulfur it contains at any given time. Intermittent geyser activity results from water seeping into fissures along the bottom of the lake, then boiling and exploding

92

upward. More likely, you'll see gas and steam escaping from fumaroles along the edge of the lake. The sides of the crater are burned and strewn with rock and ash, and only a few shrubs struggle for survival in the noxious environment at its rim.

After a visit to the active crater, climb to Laguna Botos, the water-filled extinct crater near the highest point on the volcano. The lake is named for an Indian tribe that once inhabited the area.

The last major attraction atop Poás is the nature trail, a run of about half a kilometer through a relatively undisturbed stretch of cloud forest. The signs in Spanish along the way are more poetic than informative, and some specific labels of trees and plants would be useful (says the gringo). This is the most accessible area of forest of this type in Costa Rica.

Unfortunately, it's easier to describe many of the features of Poás than actually to see them. The top of the mountain is often clouded over, at least partially. However, the clouds shift frequently. If the main crater is obscured at first, take another look before you leave. The shroud may have lifted. The view to either coast, and northward into Nicaragua, may also open up from time to time, so keep an eye peeled.

A public excursion bus to Poás leaves from the southeast corner of the central park in Alajuela on Sundays only at 9 a.m. Fare is about $3. This is an all-day excursion. The ride up takes two hours, with a twenty-minute rest stop at a café high on the volcano, near Poasito. Three hours are allowed on top before departure for Alajuela. This is more than ample time to see both accessible craters and the cloud forest. On other days, buses are available from Alajuela to San Pedro de Poás (every hour); then from San Pedro de Poás to Poasito (at 5 a.m. and 1:30 p.m.). This still leaves you 10 kilometers from the peak. You'll have to walk, hitch, or hire a taxi to finish the ascent. Tours operate to Poás most days from San José, or you can hire a taxi.

If you're driving, take the Cañas expressway to Alajuela, then follow the clearly marked route via San Pedro de Poás and Poasito. The peak is 37 kilometers from Alajuela, 59 from San José. An alternate and somewhat more arduous route from San José goes through Heredia, Barva, Los Cartagos and Poasito.

Rain gear will come in handy on Poás even in the dry season,

Oxcart Painter

when heavy winds can whip clouds across the peak. Take a sweater or jacket as well. Temperatures can dip sharply in a few minutes.

A few kilometers south of Alajuela, just east of the international airport at San Antonio de Belén, are the Ojo de Agua springs and recreation area. (This Ojo de Agua is not to be confused with the town of Ojo de Agua, west of the airport). Water gushes from the earth at a rate of 200 liters per second, and most of the flow is directed into an aqueduct that supplies the city of Puntarenas, on the Pacific.

Much of the remainder is used for the amusement of the citizenry. In the tree-shaded park surrounding the springs are three pools, tennis courts, and a lake with rowboats. On weekends, this is a great place to rub elbows and much else with the locals. Visit during the week if you prefer solitude. Entry costs about 40 cents, and changing rooms are available. There are eateries both inside and outside the gates. Through no particular logic, the recreational facilities are managed by the national railroad company.

Microbuses operate to Ojo de Agua from Calle 16, Avenidas Central /1, San José, buses from Avenida 1, Calles 18/20. There are also buses from Alajuela and Heredia. Service is more frequent on weekends.

West of Alajuela, along the highway to Atenas, at Dulce Nombre, are two specialized zoos. The Zoológico de Aves Tropicales holds an outstanding collection of tropical birds in a lovely landscaped setting. (In fact, the area around Dulce Nombre and La Garita is replete with beautiful gardens.) Usual hours are 9 a.m. to 5 p.m. daily. About 600 meters down the road, also on the right side as you come from Alajuela, is the Zoológico Tropifauna, where assorted lions, birds and apes are kept in hillside cages. Hours are 8 a.m. to 5 p.m. daily. Admission to each zoo is about 50 cents.

Both zoos make pleasant stops if you're already passing through the area, or have a special interest in tropical fauna. To reach them, take a bus for Atenas or La Garita from the terminal in Alajuela. If you're driving from San José, take the Cañas expressway to the Atenas exit, then go right for two kilometers.

West from Alajuela, the old Pan American (or Interamerican) Highway skirts the northern rim of the Central Valley, passing through the picturesque towns of Grecia, Sarchí and Naranjo. The road is in an unfortunate state of repair, and most traffic now speeds to the coast on the Bernardo Soto Expressway, to the south. But the old highway affords a pleasant, slow meander through rolling countryside.

Grecia is most notable for its unusual brick-red church. The surrounding hills here at the hotter, lower end of the central Valley are largely planted in sugarcane, and much of the output is processed in Grecia.

Beyond Grecia is Sarchí, the preeminent craft center of Costa Rica, where dozens of small wood workshops line the highway. Here, tropical hardwoods are made into chairs, tables, and, of course, the brightly-painted oxcarts with kaleidoscopic wheels for which Costa Rica is famous. The intricate painted designs on the carts are said to be handed down from father to son. These items are strictly for the local market, but the miniature oxcarts and statuettes are suitable for carrying off. The bi-towered church of Sarchí, with its unusual number of windows, is worth a glance. Costa Rica's country churches are, in general, charming, in contrast to the dull metropolitan temples.

The last major town on the Pan American Highway, before it drops to the coast, is Naranjo, dominated by a cream-colored baroque church.

Buses operate to Grecia, Sarchí and Naranjo every half hour from Alajuela, and you may return to San José by a more direct route. To continue to the coast, take a San Ramón bus from Naranjo to the Soto highway ("la pista") and flag down a bus for Puntarenas or Guanacaste.

About 48 kilometers north of Naranjo, and 95 kilometers from San José, is Ciudad Quesada (which most Costa Ricans call San Carlos), one of the gateways to the San Carlos plain, a prosperous area of increasing meat and dairy production. Ciudad Quesada is served regularly by buses from San José and Naranjo. Beyond the town, roads and bus service are poor. With a four-wheel-drive vehicle, it is possible to negotiate the dirt roads to Fortuna, near the Arenal volcano, over the Tilarán range to the new Arenal dam, and down to the Pan American Highway at Cañas.

The Other Costa Rica

Outside the Central Valley is another country, a Costa Rica that in many parts is as underdeveloped as any in Central America. Some of the differences from the highlands will be immediately apparent to the visitor. The population is generally sparse, and good roads are sparser. Houses are often ramshackle affairs, and the neat, flowered gardens around San José give way to dirt yards where chickens scratch for tidbits. The climate, of course, is generally hotter, and usually more humid.

More traditional Latin ways hold sway, in forms both attractive and difficult for the visitor to accept. Events unfold at times at a mañana pace, and schedules are an imperfectly understood concept. Warmth and hospitality are the norm, and the visitor can easily feel at home in any town where he lingers.

Other changes from the highlands are not visible, or slower to manifest themselves. The social-security system provides limited coverage outside the Central Valley, where there are fewer salaried employees. Electricity and drinkable water have not yet reached many smaller settlements. Large banana and palm plantations, cotton farms and cattle ranches take up more of the land than small family homesteads.

Progress, quite simply, is generally less than in the Central Valley, and much more uneven. There are pleasant, clean, bustling lowland towns such as Liberia; idyllic, nearly isolated national parks; and serene beach settlements. And there are places where, at first glance, the major elements of life appear to be liquor, litter and loud music.

Once you leave the main lowland routes, a flexible schedule is a must, unless you make ironclad arrangements through a travel agency. Expect simpler food and less-than-top-notch

97

service, barer hotel rooms and lower standards of hygiene. There are a few beach and mountain resorts where these cautions don't apply, but in general, more tolerance and understanding are required. Remember to phone ahead for reservations when possible, and to reconfirm schedules off the main routes, where bus service is generally poor.

The Wild East

North and east of the mountainous backbone of Costa Rica is the triangle-shaped Caribbean coastal region, a vast area of dense tropical forest. No time of year, no remote corner of the Atlantic slope, is ever dry. Clouds blow in from the sea throughout the year. Those that don't drench the area directly shed their water against the central mountains, from where it flows back to the Caribbean in numerous rivers, and often overflows onto the low-lying, poorly drained land. Rainfall at Limón, in the center of the coastal strip, reaches 150 inches in many years, and near the Nicaraguan border, approaches 200 inches.

Despite the thick layer of plants in the lowlands, the soil is poor. Enriching ash blows only westward from the volcanoes of the highlands, and constant rain leaches nutrients. The tribes that lived in this area before the Conquest were the least settled of Costa Rica, relying on hunting and gathering for their food, as well as on corn plots that had to be frequently relocated as the earth was exhausted.

The Caribbean was the locale of the first attempts by the Spaniards to conquer and settle Costa Rica. But jungle heat, endless rain, insects, poisonous tree sap, snakes, dense vegetation, yellow fever, malaria, dysentery, and a hostile population were only some of the obstacles to establishing a plantation agriculture in the region.

In the nineteenth century, as Costa Rica began to export large quantities of coffee, it became clear that a direct, all-year transport route to the Caribbean was needed. In an epic undertaking, and at a cost of thousands of lives, a railroad was completed from the port of Limón to San José in 1890. Long before that date, however, a new export crop was being carried on the route:

bananas. Costa Rica was the first nation to supply the world with the fruit, and within a few years, the crop was second only to coffee in earnings. But Panama disease ravished the plantations in the 1930s, and operations were relocated to the Pacific lowlands. Later, cacao, rubber and abaca (manila hemp) were planted in the lowlands, but none proved as profitable as bananas.

Spurred by new road and canal construction, settlements are today spreading through much of the formerly empty Caribbean region. Forests are being cut down and converted to pasture, or tilled for crops. And the once moribund banana industry is reviving, with disease-resistant varieties.

The environment in much of the Caribbean region is still largely uncomfortable, in parts threatening to human existence. Why, then, would anybody venture there, except out of necessity? The train trip to Limón, from highlands to jungle, is regarded by some as the premier travel experience in Costa Rica. The Caribbean coastline is one nearly continuous sweep of white beach, most of it deserted. Wildlife treasures abound, including green turtles in their protected nesting area at Tortuguero. Fishing, especially for tarpon, is world-famous. The blacks who form a large part of the lowland population are a fascinating culture, quite different from other Costa Ricans. And also, there is nothing menacing in those parts of the Caribbean where the visitor is likely to tread.

THE JUNGLE TRAIN

Any mention of the train ride from San José to Limón requires a preliminary excursion into some Costa Rican history. Primitive trails descended the Atlantic slope to navigable lowland rivers since early in the colonial period, but these were often made impassable by rain, and Costa Rica's limited international trade was channeled through the Pacific port of Puntarenas. As early as 1820, an improved route to the Caribbean was proposed. But no way was found to construct an all-season road, and Costa Rica's ever-expanding coffee exports continued to reach Europe only after a long detour around the tip of South America.

In 1871, the Costa Rican government contracted with Henry Meiggs, an American who had built railroads in the Andes, to

100

construct a line from Limón to San José. The work came under the supervision of a nephew of Meiggs, Minor C. Keith.

Workers were recruited, mostly from New Orleans, and financing was arranged, but the project appeared doomed almost from the beginning. Floods washed out sections of track almost as soon as they were laid. Nearly 600 of the first 700 workers were soon dead of malaria. The first 25 miles of track cost 4000 lives, mostly new Chinese recruits who succumbed to yellow fever. Keith himself lost three brothers and an uncle, but pushed on nevertheless, contracting workers from Italy and around the Caribbean. Those who survived were mostly West Indian.

Keith's credit was exhausted before the tracks had progressed far, but his men labored on for months without pay, partly out of personal loyalty, partly because there were few alternatives. Finally, Keith sought temporary revenue by planting banana shoots brought from Panama along completed sections of track. Native strains of the fruit already grew in the area, but were inedible, and left to rot. The desperate scheme was successful beyond imagination. Bananas were soon being shipped from Costa Rica, and provided more than ample funds to push on with construction over swamps, rivers and mountains.

A road was opened from San José to the railhead at Carrillo in 1882, allowing the first large-scale movement of people and goods from the highlands to the Caribbean. Landslides, floods, cave-ins and illness continued to plague the builders, but by the end of 1890, the line was open all the way from San José to Limón, a distance of 100 miles.

Meanwhile, Keith continued to expand his banana business. He was granted vast tracts of land and a 99-year lease on the railroad in exchange for completing its construction on his own account. He consolidated his holdings in Costa Rica and elsewhere into the United Fruit Company. His International Railways of Central America constructed lines throughout the isthmus.

With the completion of the railroad, the economy and face of Costa Rica were transformed. Bananas came to be almost as important as coffee to the nation's well-being. Many Jamaican laborers settled along the tracks, taking advantage of land grants under an 1884 law, or went to work on the plantations.

The railroad came under English ownership, and dominated transport in the Caribbean region until the 1970s, when an all-

The Train to Limón

weather road to Limón was completed. With containerization of ocean cargo and the increasing use of trucks, and with buses providing a more rapid passenger service, traffic has declined. Only one passenger train now operates daily in each direction between San José and Limón. The Atlantic railroad was nationalized in 1972, and turned over to JAPDEVA, the official body entrusted with the development of the Atlantic slope.

The train for Limón leaves from Avenida 3, Calle 21, San José. Tickets are sold shortly before departure time. Call 260011, extension 259, to check the schedule (recent departure time: 12 noon). The trip takes about five and a half hours.

The narrow-gauge line uses modern locomotives (an old steam engine sits in front of the station). But the cars are antiques, worn though clean, with minimally padded bench seats, painted army-green on the inside, and red, white and blue, the colors of Costa Rica, on the outside. There is usually only one class of service, but a more comfortable car is sometimes added, and may be used for an extra fee. One-way fare to Limón is less than $3. Try to get a seat on the right side of the train (leaving

102

San José) for better views.

You'll experience part of the atmosphere of Limón as soon as you board the train. Blacks from the lowlands converse with outsiders in Spanish, and with each other in their rhythmic, barely comprehensible English dialect. Occasionally you may make out a mixed English-Spanish sentence fragment, such as "Bueno, you coming Sunday too?" Vendors stalk the aisles as soon as the train gets moving (always right on time!), offering cold sodas, peanuts, potato and banana chips, and such Costa Rican goodies as empanadas (filled turnovers), enyucados (yucca cakes) and pañuelos ("handkerchiefs," a pastry) that you probably will not have found at restaurants in San José. You need not go hungry, even if you have not packed a hamper.

Immediately out of the station, the train passes by coffee plantings and pastures on undulating terrain backdropped by lush hills. Town after town after small town rolls by, near and in the distance, each dominated by its church. Rivers lined with bamboo thickets flow under the tracks. Coffee mills with concrete drying platforms, factories, grazing sheep, an oil refinery, come into and pass out of view.

An hour out of San José, past Cartago, the valley narrows, and the surrounding mountains become steeper and more dramatic, as the track follows the rocky Reventazón river, becoming a hillside clinger in stretches, curving back on itself, bridging sudden, sheer-sided canyons. In the distance, the Cachí dam may be seen, and always, the mountainsides densely carpeted with shiny-leaved coffee.

The train makes dozens of stops at apparent nowheres: no houses, no stores, no platforms await the train, just a few embarking passengers, amid bordering brush and coffee trees. Only when the train moves on do clusters of houses over a rise or down a slope come into view.

Most of the windows in the old cars will be stuck open. Dust will blow in, you will feel the increasing heat as you descend, but neither problem is insufferable. When you lean out, you will alternately brush against the leaves of trees and bushes, and suffer vertigo as the train appears to fly through thin air, on a trestle over an unseen river.

Near Turrialba, the Reventazón valley widens, as the track descends into lower country. Patches of pasture and sugar cane appear among the coffee forest, become more and more frequent, and eventually dominate, as the steeper slopes disappear. Bare patches of fill, new retaining walls, piles of rock and dirt on both sides of the track, tell of washouts and landslides.

At a distance of approximately 75 kilometers from San José (the track is well marked), coffee has given way altogether, and the land turns truly and tropically lush, the humpbacked hills covered with towering, massively trunked trees. Knowing passengers crane their necks, looking for alligators sunning on favorite rocks in the wider, lazier river. At kilometer 89 is the first of three tunnels on the line, narrow and pitch dark and a source of rollicking, whistling delight to the passengers. Keep your arms and head inside.

The town of Siquirres marks the end of the hills, and the beginning of a totally flat Costa Rica of humidity and lassitude, of ramshackle buildings peeling in the sun. Siquirres is a major railroad yard center and a junction point for the multiple roads now reaching through the lowlands, sprawling and hot, with many a second story on a building to catch whatever breeze there is.

Past Siquirres is the region first settled by Jamaican railroad and banana workers. Town after town consists of stilt wooden houses along the track, and newer brick and concrete-block houses on the dirt roads leading out to the paved highway. In overgrown yards where a few chickens scratch, and where a causeway provides a dry path when the earth is waterlogged, banana and citrus trees flourish, along with cacao trees, hardly bigger than a man, with red and yellow pods.

More interesting, though, are the people. Most of the railside towns are now well integrated, with as many Costarricense as black residents, and a few Chinese merchants. But the Jamaican flavor stands out. Blacks rock on the porches of their neat houses, women in print shifts, bandannas around their heads, men in shorts and tee-shirts. Public signs in Swampmouth, Bataan and all the other old banana settlements are in Spanish, but English holds its own on noticeboards at Protestant churches, the centers of Jamaican social life.

Nearer to the coast are fields of rice, and, in parts, nothing but bananas as far as the eye can see. Five hours out of San José, after Matina, the track takes a turn southward, and runs through coconut groves along mile after mile of near-deserted beach. The idyll lasts a half-hour, until the oil-storage tanks of Moín come into view. A few minutes later, a shantytown of stilt swamp-houses is the first sight of Limón.

On arrival in Limón, you're faced with a few choices. Most obviously, you can head to town (turn right from the station onto the main street, then walk seven blocks to the main square), check into a hotel, and spend a few days exploring the coast to the north or south. Or you can stay over and return by train to San José—the view is different going up. If you're short of time, buses are available for an immediate return to San José. There are also daily flights, but schedules do not currently mesh with train arrivals. Check with SANSA airlines in San José if you wish to return the next day by air, and reserve.

Travel agencies in San José offer tours that will take you part of the way to Limón on the jungle train, then back to San José by bus.

LIMON

Population: 43,500; Altitude: 3 meters; 168 kilometers from San José.

Limón, Costa Rica's main Caribbean port, opened to banana traffic in 1880, but its place in national history is more venerable. Christopher Columbus landed offshore, at Uvita Island, in 1502. The first Spanish attempts at settlement were made in the area. Intermittently through the colonial period, encounters with the British and Dutch, both commercial and bellicose, took place at Portete, just a few kilometers to the north.

The port city of Limón that grew with the railway was as much a part of the British West Indies as of Costa Rica. Blacks from Jamaica and other islands constituted most of the popula-tion, and English was the only language that mattered in business. Immigrant workers kept their British passports, sent their chil-dren to school in English, read Jamaican newspapers, and went to the movies to see British films. Limón and the banana lands were separated from Costa Rica not only by language and culture, but also by a law that forbade blacks from crossing the Central

Valley or spending a night there.

The separate society of the lowlands began to break down in the 1930s, when the banana industry was uprooted by Panama disease, and relocated to the Pacific lowlands. After the civil war of 1949, blacks were granted full citizenship, and in small numbers began to migrate to the Central Valley. Meanwhile, more and more Costa Ricans of the overcrowded plateau looked for opportunities in the warm country to the east. Most black children were educated in Spanish after 1949, and the use of English has been declining since.

Limón today is a mixed Hispanic and Afro-Caribbean city, but more and more, the Hispanic predominates. The local Jamaican patois, permeated with Spanish words, is the language of the older generation. Nevertheless, Afro-Caribbean ways hold on. Columbus Day is celebrated in Limón as it is throughout Latin America, but with a fervor and style that correspond to those of Carnival in the islands. Home cooking, heavy on fish, tripe, rice, coconut, and stews with cow's feet, is less than familiar to other Costa Ricans. Religion is a vibrant part of the lives of the black population, and not the formality that it is to the broad class of Hispanic Costa Ricans.

People rise early in Limón to beat the heat, go about their business, then take a long break until the worst of the sun is gone. Businesses stay open late, and music blares on all streets from record shops, bars and restaurants. The sounds are Latin and Soul, reflecting the population division. Sailors, hangers-on and prostitutes frequent the bars, many of them open 24 hours. The best show in Limón is the street life, the commerce and hustling in the market and open squares, and under the concrete overhangs on all the main streets.

To the visitor, Limón at first glance is probably a disappointment, rich in culture and tradition, but run down. Fruit and sodden garbage sometimes rot in the streets waiting for a tardy pickup, buildings decay in the salt air, ironwork balconies and tin roofs rust away. But appearance is a relative matter. Compared to the towns of the Central Valley, Limón is shabby. Compared to other ports on this coast—Belize City, Puerto Barrios in Guatemala, La Ceiba in Honduras—Limón is pristine with its paved streets, functioning sewers, a clean market. Of teeming tropical ports, it is a good choice for the outsider to sample. But if people-watching in a throbbing, hot town is not your cup of tea, move on to the beaches and parks to the north or south.

Orientation

Avenida 2 is Limón's main street, running east from the railway passenger station to Vargas Park, near the waterfront. Avenidas 3, 4, 5, etc., run parallel to Avenida 2, and north of it. (There is no odd-even segregation, as in San José). Calle 1 runs north-south at Vargas Park. The higher-numbered calles are to the west, toward the passenger station. The freight line of the railroad, running to the docks, bounds Limón to the south, along Avenida 1.

Though all streets have numbers, you won't find them posted anywhere. Locals use their own tags—Avenida 2 is the Market Street. Memorize where key points are—the market is along Avenida 2, between Calles 3 and 4—or else ask directions shamelessly.

Hotels

There are no first-rate establishments in Limón, but you can spend a comfortable night at a reasonable price.

Hotel Acón, Calle 3, Avenida 3, tel. 581010. 39 rooms. $16 single/$20 double.

Best in town, despite plain, bare rooms and washbasins that drain into the showers. Clean and air-conditioned.

Hotel Internacional, Calle 3, Avenida 5, tel. 580434. 20 rooms. $8/$13.

Relatively new, with air conditioning, plain rooms. Good buy.

Hotel Las Olas, Portete, tel. 581414. 52 rooms. Weekdays, $14/ $18; Weekends, $20/$27.

Located a couple of kilometers north of Limón, right at the water's edge. Air-conditioned, clean rooms; caters to weekenders from San José. Take a taxi to get here after dark, or the Moín bus during daylight hours.

Hotel Miami, Avenida 2, Calles 4/5, tel. 580490. 12 rooms. $9/
$14.

One of the first hotels you come to on the main street, walking
from the railroad station. Bare and peeling rooms, but with air
conditioning.

Hotel Park, Avenida 3, Calles 1/2, tel. 580476. 14 rooms. $8/
$13.

Limón's dowager hotel, once the best in town, with restaurant,
bar, good views of the port, simple but adequate rooms, and an
aura of faded glory. Nice, if you can do without air conditioning.

Hotel Lincoln, Avenida 5, Calles 2/3, tel. 580074. $4 per person.

Plain, fans available.

Hotel Cariari, Calle 2, Avenidas 2/3, tel. 581395. 7 rooms. $2
per person.

Bare, hot.

Other lodgings are available around Playa Bonita, five kilometers north of Limón. These are mentioned below.

Food
With the sea nearby, lobster and shrimp cost slightly less in
Limón than in San José, so you may be tempted to try them.
Another specialty of the town is Jamaican-style cooking, but
unfortunately, it's a home phenomenon that only rarely makes
its way to restaurant menus. In general, you can eat wholesomely
and heartily in Limón, but not exquisitely.

The best restaurant in town is in the best hotel, the Acón.
"Best" in this case means simple food in a comfortable, air-conditioned dining room. The menu has the usual assortment of
chicken, beef and fish main courses for $4 to $5, American
breakfasts for $3.

The restaurant at the Hotel Internacional offers similar fare
to the Acón's, with slightly lower prices, as well as some shrimp
and lobster dishes for $7.50 and up. The best selections, though,
are Chinese. A *cho min* with mushrooms, ham and tiny shrimp

108

costs $3.

The American Bar is the liveliest place in Limón, an open-to-the-street place at Calle 1 and Avenida 2, opposite Vargas Park. Good for seafood (shrimp $5, lobster $10) and beef ($3) if you like large portions and don't fuss about preparation. Sailors and available women and persons on extended visits and even a few locals hang out here, more for the booze than the food.

Also active are the Bar Internacional, Calle 4 and Avenida 3, and the Springfield, on the northern edge of town. And you'll have no trouble finding additional drinking spots in Limón.

For the cheapest meals, try rubbing elbows with the locals at the eateries inside the market buildings.

Transport

The most famous way to get to Limón is via the train, described above. Departures for San José are currently at 6 a.m. from the passenger station, at Avenida 2, Calle 8. Faster buses (four to five hours) leave every hour from 6 a.m. to 6 p.m. from Avenida 3, Calles 19/21, San José. Return buses leave on the same schedule from Avenida 2, Calle 2, Limón. Fastest service is by plane. SANSA currently has flights from San José at 10:30 a.m. and 3 p.m., every day except Sunday. Flights to San José depart most days at 11:30 a.m. and 4 p.m. In addition, there are flights on Mondays and Fridays from Limón to Barra del Colorado at 3:30 p.m. The airport is located three kilometers south of Limón along the coast road. Telephone the local SANSA agency at 580241.

Around Limón

The favorite place for sitting down in Limón is Vargas Park, a square of jungle at Avenida 2 and Calle 1, facing the sea. Giant hardwoods struggle against the odds with strangler figs, huge palms shoot toward the sky, vines and bromeliads compete for space and moisture, birds dart and flit through the tangle. There are supposed to monkeys and three-toed sloths up there somewhere in the canopy, and perhaps you'll be luckier than me and spy them.

Across from the park is Limon's perfect tropical-port city hall, with its cream-colored stucco, open arcades and breezeways, balconies, and louvered windows. Limon's older architecture is well suited to the climate. Thick walls moderate the extremes of temperature, concrete overhangs block the sun and keep people dry when it rains, as it does drenchingly often.

The market, on Avenida 2 between Calles 3 and 4, is ever lively, set back in a large building in its own little park. Stop in and admire the papaya and passionfruit (granadilla), as well as the more mundane but no less impressive one-pound carrots. The streets around the market are Limon's social center, where purveyors of food and games of chance set up shop during the Columbus Day celebrations and for the month preceding Christmas. The Columbus Day "carnival" season features floats, street bands, dancing and masquerades, and everything else that one expects to find in the islands at Mardi Gras.

Along the southern rim of Limón (Avenida 1) are the railroad tracks and the piers where bananas are loaded aboard ship. Despite the long journey to markets all over the world, bananas are delicate. In hot weather, the large leaves of the plant collapse to shelter the fruit. In dry spells, the pores contract to conserve water. Once the stems with their "hands" (rows) of "fingers" (individual fruits) are cut from the plant, natural defenses are gone, and the fruit is rushed from the field to cooled ship's hold in 18 hours. The plants are chopped down after harvest, but new plants grow up from suckers and bear fruit in nine to fourteen months. Watch the banana loading from a distance, if you can and while you can. More and more, the fruit is loaded into cargo containers right after cutting, minimizing damage from excessive handling. With advanced cultivation techniques, Costa Rica's banana fields have the highest yields in Latin America.

It is the Latins in Limón who stay up late and party. The bars open at 8 a.m. and soon people are bending elbows. Blacks, religious Protestants most of them, go family-style to the numerous and substantial churches.

Try to catch and understand snatches of Limón English. Many a word is different from what you know, and the rhythms and speech patterns further obscure what is said. Most confusing is that many of the words are not English at all, but Spanish, notably the numbers. Most of Limón's blacks can also speak a more standard form of English that you'll find intelligible in direct conversation.

Limón is located on a rocky point, and is one of the few

places along Costa Rica's Caribbean coast without a beach. There's a government-sponsored pool in town, but most visitors will prefer the nearby beaches.

North of Limón

Several beaches north of Limón are play areas for people from the area and for weekenders from San José. Playa Bonita is a public park about four kilometers from Limón, with an absolutely idyllic bay, plenty of lush jungle vegetation as a backdrop, and a beach that attracts quite a share of debris. Facilities are limited—a few picnic tables and a children's play area.

Portete, a little cove full of fishing boats, adjoins Playa Bonita to the north. You can sit at the many little stands that serve food and watch as lobster traps are prepared, or just stare at the sea or the jungle and coconut trees. The shore is rocky and littered.

All around Playa Bonita and Portete are a number of beach houses, and a few places offering accommodations to transients. Bare beach *cabinas,* usually little more than cubicles, are available starting from $3 per person per day, just south of Playa Bonita park. The Hotel Matama (tel. 581123) rents out furnished bungalows in a nicely lush hillside setting, but otherwise has limited facilities—a swimming pool that may or may not be full, and a restaurant. The bungalows go for $52 per day for any number of persons.

The public bus for Playa Bonita, Portete and Moín runs every hour from Calle 4, Avenida 4 in Limón, in front of Radio Casino.

TORTUGUERO CANAL

Moín, seven kilometers from Limón, is hardly a town at all, but rather a transport center. All of Costa Rica's oil supplies are off-loaded here, and stored in huge tanks.

More interestingly, Moín is also the passenger and freight terminal for the Canal de Tortuguero, the 160-kilometer stretch of natural rivers, lagoons and estuaries, and connecting man-made waterways, that runs almost to the Nicaraguan border. The canal is the main "highway" of the northern coastal region, complete with directional signs and branches from the main trunk route. Cargo and passengers move on narrow, tuglike, 30-foot-long launches. Ask permission to enter the compound of JAPDEVA, the government agency in charge of economic development in the area, to take a look at river port operations. Coconuts, bamboo, cacao and bananas are unloaded, and consumer goods, largely bottled sodas, are loaded for the return run. From the terminal, you can see the stately waterway, thick with water lilies, its banks lined with vine-entangled trees, dissolving in the distance into swamps.

To ride on the canal, you have a number of choices, not all of them convenient. Cargo-and-passenger boats operate on an irregular basis to Parismina, Tortuguero and Barra del Colorado. Those going to Tortuguero usually leave at about 7 a.m., and charge from $3 to $5 for the eight-hour trip. You could then stay over in Tortuguero, where basic accommodations are available, and either continue to Barra del Colorado or return to Moín. Get to Moín early, or go out the day before to try to arrange your trip with one of the boat captains. You may have to sit atop the cargo, but you will be well rewarded with views of pastel-colored toucans and macaws, monkeys swinging through the trees, sloths hanging from branches, alligators taking the sun, and perhaps some of the coatis, jaguars and ocelots that roam the forest. Scattered along the way are people, too—fishermen and farmers whose dugouts serve all the purposes of pickup trucks elsewhere. Knots of women washing clothes and clusters of thatched huts show that the canal is serving its purpose of bringing settlement to the area. But mostly, the banks remain wild, and the screams of monkeys and whistles of birds predominate over the noises of humans. Riding a canal boat is probably the easiest way that exists of penetrating the tropical rain forest.

Japdeva also sometimes runs its own launch from Moín, with lower fares. Phone 581106 or inquire at the river port for information. There are, as well, more comfortable and more reliable ways of cruising the canal, but they cost more. The Río Colorado Lodge (Box 5094, San José, tel. 324063) offers a $200 package that includes bus transportation to Moín, a cruise through the canal to Barra del Colorado, a night's lodging, and return by air to San José. Similar arrangements are available from most travel agents in San José. Or, you can attempt to charter a boat for a ride from Moín according to your own schedule. However, traffic on the canal is sparse and irregular, and without advance arrange-

112

ments through a travel agency, you can't count on anything. When locals can't find a boat, they simply walk along the beach—six hours to Parismina, twelve or more to Tortuguero—and count on friendly dugout owners to take them across intervening estuaries.

TORTUGUERO NATIONAL PARK

Located eighty kilometers north of Limón, Tortuguero National Park is most famed for the nesting sea turtles that give their name to both the park and adjacent town. Every year from June to November, turtles waddle ashore at night, climb past the high-tide line, excavate cavities in the sand and lay their eggs, then crawl off, exhausted.

Only fifty years ago, the waves of turtles were so dense that one turtle would often dig out the eggs of another in the process of making its nest. The eggs were gathered by locals almost as soon as they were deposited, and enjoyed great popularity not only as a food, but because of their alleged aphrodisiac powers. The turtles, too, were often overturned and disemboweled for their meat and shell. Now, depredations by humans have reached such an extent that the survival of some species is in doubt.

Tortuguero is one of the few remaining nesting places of the green Atlantic turtle, a species that reaches a meter in length and 200 kilograms in weight. Green turtle eggs are deposited from August to November every three years. Other species that nest at the beach are the hawksbill, loggerhead, and the huge leatherback, which weights up to 700 kilograms.

Even with human enemies under control in the park, the turtle eggs, slightly smaller than those of hens, face numerous perils. Raccoons, coatis and coyotes dig them out and eat them up. The hatchlings that emerge two months after laying face a run for the sea made perilous by crabs and lizards, and birds that swoop down and pluck off tasty morsels of leg or head. Only a small fraction of hatchlings reaches the sea, and fewer still make it to adulthood. The odds are being improved somewhat by programs that see to the safe transfer of hatchlings to the water.

Visitors come to Tortuguero to witness the nighttime nesting of the turtles, but the park is also an important conservation area for other plant and animal species, as much of the tropical forest nearby is cut down and otherwise disturbed by humans. Freshwater turtles, manatees and alligators are found in the canals of the park, as well as sport fish and fresh-water sharks that reach up to three meters in length. Forest animals include the jaguar, tapir, anteater, ocelot, howler and spider monkeys, kinkajou, cougar, collared peccary, white-lipped peccary, and coatimundi. Over 300 bird species have been reported in the park, including the endangered green macaw, Central American curassow and yellowtailed oriole.

All of Tortuguero is wet—rainfall averages 5000 millimeters (200 inches) per year—but there are several vegetation zones. Morning glory vines, coconut palms and shrubs characterize the sandy beach area, while other sectors are covered with swampy forest. In the forest on higher, less saturated ground, orchids and bromeliads live at all levels and take their nourishment from the air, and "exotic" houseplant species, such as dieffenbachia, flourish.

Visiting Tortuguero

The park service requests notification in advance from visitors, though I don't know of anyone being turned away for having showed up unannounced. However, if you're planning an overnight stay, it would be wise to check with the park service, since facilities are limited. Camping is permitted, and a few rooms are available in the town of Tortuguero, which contains about a dozen houses and less than a hundred inhabitants, most of them English-speaking. To make reservations and inquire about prices, phone 718099. The Tortuga Lodge, three kilometers north of Tortuguero, provides rooms with private bath, meals, and boats for fishing or exploring the waterways of the park. Phone 338108 in San José, or 716861 to reach the lodge directly. Boats are available for hire in the town of Tortuguero as well.

Getting to Tortuguero is not easy unless you charter a private plane to the beach landing strip, three miles to the north. From Moín, north of Limón, you can try to board one of the canal launches heading north. The trip takes about eight hours, but you can't tell in advance on which day you'll be able to travel. A last alternative is to fly from San José to Barra del Colorado, 35 kilometers north of Tortuguero, and hire a boat to the park, a trip of three to four hours. Tours of the Tortuguero Canal pass through the park, of course, but they don't pause in the evening, when turtles nest.

BARRA DEL COLORADO

The Tortuguero Canal terminates at the settlement of Barra del Colorado, which sits astride the mouth of the Colorado River, a delta branch of the San Juan River that borders Nicaragua. Barra prospered in the forties as a lumber center and depot for cargo coming downriver from Nicaragua. But as woodcutting and river trade declined, so did Barra's fortunes. The population is now down to a few hundred, many of Nicaraguan descent.

Barra serves today as a takeoff point for visiting Tortuguero Park, and as a sport fishing center. But it also has its attractions as an out-of-the-way place with a friendly populace, where one can stay on the edge of the wild in relative comfort.

Small planes operate twice weekly between Barra and San José (current departures for San José Monday and Friday at 4:45 p.m., via Limon; from San José the same days at 3 p.m.). Private boats may be hired for jungle cruises in the vicinity, or for trips to Tortuguero Park. More adventurously, small cargo boats operate irregularly up the San Juan and Sarapiquí rivers to Puerto Viejo, which is tied by road with Heredia and San José. One can try to ship on a boat going upriver to complete an overland circle trip, but not if time is important: departures are always uncertain on these back river routes.

The wide San Juan lies entirely in Nicaragua, but Costa Rica enjoys full rights to use the river. More than a hundred years ago, Cornelius Vanderbilt established a combination riverboat-ferry-stage coach service that used the San Juan as part of a passenger route across Nicaragua, connecting with steamers from both coasts of the States. The service was disrupted during William Walker's takeover in Nicaragua, and as part of the post-war settlement, Costa Rica pushed its border north to the banks of the river. Panama thereafter dominated interoceanic transport, though the San Juan has been proposed from time to time as part of a new canal. The most famous navigators hereabouts nowadays are the sharks that move between Lake Nicaragua, upstream on the San Juan, and the Caribbean. Sharks frequent the coast down to Tortuguero as well, feeding on the abundant fish and making swimming one of the less peaceful diversions available.

Accommodations

Río Colorado Lodge. 12 rooms. $100 per person with meals, use of boats, and guides.

San José office: **Hotel Corobici,** tel. 328610. U.S. address: P.O. Box 11168, Jacksonville, FL 32239, tel. 904-744-4213.

Simple but comfortable screened cabins. This is mainly a fishing lodge, but the friendly management also organizes excursions through the Tortuguero Canal and welcomes non-sportsmen to beachcomb and relax on the edge of the jungle. A mini-zoo on the grounds holds animals from the area. The food is said to be good.

There is one other place to stay in Barra, a pension with basic rooms for about $4 per person.

FISHING ALONG THE CARIBBEAN

Although remote, the Caribbean coast of Costa Rica is world famous for sport fishing. Tarpon, or sábalo, is the most notable (or notorious) species, most easily found from January to June, with March and April the best months (though tarpon habits are unpredictable). Tarpon generally weigh from 60 to 100 pounds.

Second to the tarpon as a sport fish is snook (róbalo), generally caught from mid-August to mid-October, and averaging over 25 pounds. Other species are snapper (pargo), machaca, guapote, bass, mojarra and jacks, which generally run under five pounds.

Almost all the fishing along the coasts is in fresh-water river estuaries and lagoons, which at times are converted into furious cauldrons of spawning fish. At the right times, not having a good catch is virtually impossible. Fishing in the open waters of the Caribbean is a risky business, due to the unpredictability of

116

winds and storms.

In addition to the Río Colorado lodge, the following fishing camps are located along the Caribbean:

Tarpon Rancho, near Parismina (40 kilometers north of Limón). 10 rooms, approximately $150 per person per day.

San José address: P. O. Box 5712. U. S. address: The Piers, 1313 Cass Lane East, Westmont, IL 60559, tel. 312-963-7541.

One of the longest-established fishing camps in the Caribbean, located on the edge of an isolated village. Two world records for snook have been set here. Rooms are basic and clean, in wooden cottages, and food is plentiful. Fishing is from 16-foot aluminum skiffs, with guides provided. Open January to May and August to October.

Isla de Pesca, near Barra del Colorado. 12 units, approximately $200 per day, all-inclusive.

Reservations: Fishing Travel, 2525 Nevada Ave. N., Golden Valley, MN 55427, tel. 612-541-1088.

This lodge is highly rated for its clean accommodations and good food. Cottages are simple, with full bathrooms. Fishing is from 16-foot skiffs. Rates include the flight from San José to Barra, as well as use of boat and guides, and meals.

South of Limón

The coast to the south of Limón, as to the north, is a nearly continuous stretch of sandy, idyllic, usually deserted beach. There are a few differences, however. Rainfall is lower to the south, and the terrain is generally better drained. This gives the landscape a less jungly nature, and makes it more habitable. It also makes things easier for the visitor, though you will be inevitably rained upon. Transport to the south is better developed as well. An unpaved road runs down the coast to Puerto Viejo, a branch road reaches Sixaola on the Panamanian border, and rail lines and spurs serve the banana operations of the area. The

117

region is still sparsely settled, however, with many kilometers between settlements, and few places where a visitor may stop for the night.

South from Limón, the main road generally hugs the coast and beach. Visitors may take a bus and get off at any point that looks attractive for swimming and sunning. Landward, scrub vegetation alternates with cattle pastures and coconut plantations. About 30 kilometers from Limón, the road starts to run back a couple of kilometers from the sea. A branch road goes up the valley of the Estrella River, where a revival of banana cultivation is under way. 43 kilometers from Limón is the town of Cahuita.

CAHUITA NATIONAL PARK

Cahuita National Park has beaches as beautiful as any on the Caribbean, and a few additional distinctions. Just offshore is a living coral reef, the most accessible in Costa Rica, where brightly colored fish feed and breed. In the marshes and forests of the park, animal and bird life are abundant.

The coral reef, which consists of the remains of small animals called polyps, lies up to half a kilometer from shore, and from one to seven meters under the surface. With diving equipment (none is available for rent at the park), you can see the formations—brain, elkhorn, star and dozens of other corals—as well as the fish, sponges, crabs and snails that are attracted to feed and live on the reef. At two points on the reef's western side, cannonballs, anchors, cannon and bricks have been found, giving evidence that a Spanish galleon (or more than one) sank in these waters.

In the reef-protected shallows of Cahuita, sargasso and other grasses flourish, along with conch and ghost crabs. Dead trunks of trees lie just under the water, penetrated by seawood borers, the termites of the sea.

Beyond the reef at the south end of the park, Cahuita's lovely beach, beaten by huge waves, backed by coconut palms, is a nesting site for green, Hawksbill and leatherback turtles. The gentle sweep of the bay is quite unusual on this coast. In some

118

sections, little pools form at low tide, temporarily isolating fish.

Inland, Cahuita's protected area includes extensive areas of marsh. The Perezoso (Sloth) River that flows to the sea in the park is dark brown in color, said to be an effect of the high tannin concentration, which also reputedly keeps a cap on the local mosquito population. The forests are alive with howler monkeys, white-faced monkeys, three-toed sloths, anteaters, and collared peccaries. Raccoons and coatis are often seen along the nature trail, which penetrates the damp world of ferns and bromeliads and huge jungle trees.

The town of Cahuita, at the northern end of the park, provides limited accommodations. Best of a few small hotels is the Hotel Cahuita (tel. 581515, extension 201), where the rate is about $4 per person. There are a number of small diners as well. The southern entrance to the park is about six kilometers farther on, at Puerto Vargas (Vargas Harbour). Here the park administration, nature trail and camping facilities are located.

If you plan to snorkel, you'll find the water clearest from February through April, when it rains the least. The park is usually nearly deserted, except on weekends and at holiday periods.

Buses for Sixaola pass both entrances to Cahuita Park. Departures are from Limón (Avenida 4, Calle 3) at 5 a.m., 10 a.m., 1 p.m. and 4 p.m. The rickety buses are usually crowded, so arrive at the station early to get a seat. It takes about an hour and a half to get to the town of Cahuita.

Buses also provide service to Bribri, Puerto Viejo and Sixaola. Bribri, 65 kilometers from Limón, includes in its population a number of Indians, and there are other, more remote Indian centers farther inland. Puerto Viejo (Old Harbour) is along a nice stretch of beach, and offers basic accommodations. One can easily make a trip from Limón to Puerto Viejo into a day outing. Sixaola is the crossing point to the isolated northwest region of Panama. No roads continue to the rest of Panama from this area, but flights are available to David, and onward to Panama City.

Up and Down the Pacific

Pacific Costa Rica covers a vast sweep of territory along the wide side of the country, from Nicaragua down to the Panamanian border. Overlooking a complicated, varied terrain are the volcanoes and mountain peaks of the Guanacaste, Tilaran and Talamanca mountain ranges, which largely block the rains that blow across Costa Rica from the Caribbean. Winds blow on shore from the west from May through October, bringing storms to the area, while the rest of the year is dry. But there are exceptions. The Guanacaste lowlands of the northeast, hemmed in by coastal mountains, are subject to periodic droughts. In the south, on the other hand, near Golfito, the coastal mountains act as a watershed, and it rains throughout the year. In general, rainfall, humidity and discomfort increase toward the south. The daytime temperature throughout the area is generally in the nineties Fahrenheit (32°-37° centigrade).

The central part of the coastal region is a narrow plain, broken by rivers that drip down over rocky beds from the highlands in the dry season and rush down in torrents during the rainy months. Farther to the north, the plain widens into the savanna of Guanacaste, a former forest area that lost its natural cover as it was turned into farm and grazing land. A rocky fringe borders the sparsely populated Nicoya peninsula, in the north, along the sea. Barely settled at all is the Osa peninsula, in the southern part of the region.

Travel to the main towns in the northern part of the Pacific coastal region—Puntarenas, Cañas, Liberia—is made easy by an excellent highway and frequent bus service. Most of the main attractions of the coastal region—notably the best beaches—are off this route, however, and are reached with difficulty on poor roads.

120

PUNTARENAS

Population: 38,750; Altitude: 3 meters; 112 kilometers from San José.

Puntarenas is one miles-long sandspit (which is what its name means), sticking out into the Gulf of Nicoya, a narrow, muddy estuary on one side, clear water on the other. Opened to shipping in 1814, the port was for many years Costa Rica's only outlet to world commerce. The coffee crop moved down to the coast from the highlands on oxcarts with a legendary breed of driver, rough and ready, but scrupulously honest. Today, Puntarenas is still one of the larger cities in the country, and a major shipping terminal. Trains and trucks arrive frequently with goods, and the streets are choked with commerce.

The location of Puntarenas is strategic for the visitor. The ferries that depart from here provide the easiest access to some of the nicer beaches on the Nicoya peninsula. Cruises from the yacht club touch the many islands in the Gulf of Nicoya. Puntarenas is the nearest Pacific point to San José.

Unfortunately, though, much of the city is a dump. I don't mean only that the beach is dirty for its whole great length along the south side of town, though it is. The central part of the city consists of dismal, rotting and rusting, ramshackle structures, cheap flophouses, bar after bar oozing drunks, and streets strewn with garbage and emitting a stench into the humid, dense air that will make you gag.

Not that all of Puntarenas is hard to take. There are some nice residences near the western tip of town, a few good hotels, and a substantial yacht club. The headquarters of the port, at the main pier, are in a lovely old building. Eating in the open-air diners along the beach and mixing with the crowds that come down for the day from San José can be pleasant. But Costa Rica has much nicer seaside places to offer, and you didn't come all the way from home to hang out here.

Hotels
Because Puntarenas is so accessible from San José, hotels are overpriced for what they offer.

121

Motel Tioga, Paseo de los Turistas (Avenida 4, beach side, ten blocks west of the large pier), tel. 610271. 46 rooms. $24 single/ $37 double.

Nice rooms, many with views to the sea, well-maintained, air-conditioned. Best of the in-town lodgings. There's a pool, and a restaurant offers good fresh fish as well as meat and chicken dishes at $4 to $5 for an entree. Rates include full breakfast in the fourth-floor dining-room-with-a-view.

Hotel Cayuga, Calle 4, Avenidas Central /1 (one block north of the microwave tower), tel. 610344. 31 rooms. $10 per person.

Located near the center of town, which is unfortunate, because this is the best hotel buy in Puntarenas, clean, modern, with a decent restaurant (entrees $3 to $4) and air conditioning.

Hotel Las Hamacas, Paseo de los Turistas (Avenida 4), Calles 5/7, tel. 610398. 25 rooms. $11/$18.

Quite visible with its compound facing the beach, but a last choice among the centrally located hotels, with hospital-type rooms and no hot water.

Various "cabinas" (simple rooms with few facilities) are also available at locations along the beachfront, at prices of about $6 to $8 per person.

Hotel Porto Bello, Avenida 1, Calles 72/74, tel. 321248, 610833. 34 rooms. $65/$75.

Located a safe few miles from the center of Puntarenas in its own nicely landscaped compound, attractive Mediterranean-style construction, recently renovated, air-conditioned, t.v. in some rooms, pool, private beach. The brochure advertises "childish service." (They mean baby-sitters. The service is okay.)

Costa Rica Yacht Club, three kilometers from the center of Puntarenas, tel. 610784 (in San José: P. O. Box 2530, tel. 223818). $35 per unit.

Full docking facilities, with food and fuel supply, as well as a hotel open to non-members. Rooms are comfortable, cabins will sleep up to six in marine-style, tight quarters.

Restaurants
You can try the restaurants at the hotels in town, but the most fun, and the freshest fish, are at the open-air eating places along the beach, near the main pier.

Transportation
Buses for Puntarenas leave from Calle 12, Avenida 9, San José, every hour from 6 a.m. to 6 p.m. The trip takes about two hours. In Puntarenas, buses for San José leave from Calle 2 and Avenida 4, one block east (toward the mainland) from the main pier.

Trains for Puntarenas leave from the station at Calle 2, Avenida 20, San José, at 6:30 a.m. and 3 p.m. Take the Paso Ancho bus from the main square to the station. The trip takes four hours, follows a different route from the highway, and is quite scenic. Trains for San José depart at 6 a.m. and 3 p.m. To travel south along the coast from Puntarenas, take the train to Orotina, then a bus south to Jacó, Quepos, or wherever you are going.

Buses depart for various nearby towns from the vicinity of the market, which is along the northern (estero, or estuary) side of downtown. The bus for Monteverde leaves at 2:15 p.m. from in front of the Cine Oriental, a block north (toward the estuary) from the microwave tower.

Swimming
Since the beach at Puntarenas isn't inviting, you may want to look for other swimming opportunities. The boats mentioned below will take you to some nice beaches on the Nicoya Peninsula. Nearer to Puntarenas, the best swimming is at Doña Ana beach, out of town on the road south to Caldera. A campground, restaurant, bar and changing rooms are available, but there is no easy way to reach the beach except by car or taxi.

Boats from Puntarenas
Really, the only reason for a foreign visitor to go to Puntarenas is to leave promptly for some of the nicer places along the coast.

Many are accessible by boat, either directly or in combination with car or bus travel.

A passenger and automobile ferry operates daily between Puntarenas and Playa Naranjo, on the Nicoya Peninsula. Departures from Puntarenas are at 7 a.m. and 4 p.m., from the dock at Calle 29 and Avenida 3, on the estuary side near the western end of the peninsula. The ferry leaves Playa Naranjo at 9 a.m. and 6 p.m. Fare is about $1 for passengers. From December through April, there's an extra daily trip on Friday, Saturday and Sunday from Puntarenas at 11 a.m., and from Playa Naranjo at 1 p.m. Basic restaurant service is available on board. Phone 611069 to confirm schedules.

The Playa Naranjo ferry provides a shortcut to the southern part of the Nicoya peninsula. Buses going to the town of Nicoya meet the ferry, but public transport to other towns is hard to find. Playa Naranjo is a dock and little else, but one of the nicer hotels in the peninsula, the Oasis del Pacífico, is just a few hundred meters down the road (see description in coverage of Nicoya Peninsula, below).

A passenger-only boat for Paquera, also in the Nicoya Peninsula, leaves daily at 6 a.m. from the broken-down dock ("la muellecita") behind the market in Puntarenas (Calle 2, on the estuary side). Fare is less than a dollar. Buses provide onward transportation from Paquera to Tambor and Cóbano.

On Sundays only, a boat leaves at 9 a.m. for El Coro beach on San Lucas Island, halfway across the gulf. Departure for Puntarenas is at 2 p.m.

The Yacht Calypso makes a daily cruise from the yacht club to seven islands in the Gulf of Nicoya. Fare is $38, or $49 if you book from San José and overland transportation is included. Drinks are served on board, and the longest stop is at Jesusita Island, where lunch is served. This cruise may be booked through any hotel in Puntarenas.

Arrangements may also be made with private boat owners at the docks in Puntarenas to visit the islands in the Gulf of Nicoya. On Chira, the largest, near the northern end of the gulf, cattle are raised and salt is extracted from sea water. Guayabo, Negritos and Los Pájaros islands are biological reserves, noted for their abundance of seabirds. Cedros and several smaller islands have no restaurants, hotels or any other facilities, and few inhabitants, but are excellent locales for bird watching.

On Jesusita island, the small (20-room) Hotel Isla Jesusita provides a relaxed, away-from-it-all atmosphere. The main activities are lying in a hammock and sunbathing, though boats for fishing and water skiing are available. Rate is $100 single or double with meals, and the food is said to be quite good. Phone 610263 to reserve and make travel arrangements in Costa Rica.

North from Puntarenas

The main coastal highway runs north through the rolling coastal plain from outside Puntarenas, passing through Cañas, and then over flat country to Bagaces and Liberia. None of these places is of much interest to visitors. But off the road, and accessible from it, are some of the natural wonders for which Costa Rica is known.

MONTEVERDE

High on the ridge above the coastal plain are the town of Santa Elena, and the adjacent farming colony and cloud-forest reserve of Monteverde. Costa Rica is rich in montane tropical rain forest of the type included in the Monteverde reserve—the forest atop the volcano Poás is one example, and is much more accessible. But the slow ascent to Monteverde offers spectacular views, the rolling, pastured countryside is idyllic and even spiritually uplifting, and the reserve is large. The inns in the area invite the visitor to linger and explore the forest, or relax in the fresh mountain air.

The Monteverde farming colony was founded on April 19, 1951, by Quakers from Alabama, some of whom had been imprisoned for refusing to serve in the U. S. armed forces. There were only oxcart trails into the area at the time, and the trucks and tractors of the settlers had to be winched up the mountains. Land was laboriously cleared, and the colony eventually found some prosperity in dairy farming. Monteverde cheeses now have a solid share of the Costa Rican cheese market. Over the years, the settlement changed, as some of the original families moved on, while non-Quakers bought land in the area. Monteverde is now a mixed, largely English-speaking community.

The original settlers set aside 2500 hectares of land to protect the native plant life, even as it was being destroyed by clearing in other parts of the colony. A private foundation, the Tropical Science Center, now administers the reserve. Government protection has been afforded to the rare species found at Monteverde, including the golden toad (sapo dorado), which is known to live only in rainpools in the area. The original acreage has been expanded by the purchase of adjacent lands, some of which had been farmed but are now being allowed to return to their natural state.

Getting to Monteverde

A bus operates daily from Puntarenas to the town of Santa Elena, six kilometers from the reserve. Departure is from the Cine Oriental, a block north of the microwave tower, at 2:15 p.m. Departure from Santa Elena for Puntarenas is at 6 a.m. Buses on this route are of the uncomfortable school-bus type that serves the back roads of Costa Rica. To connect with the Monteverde bus, take the train from San José (Calle 2, Avenida 20) at 6:30 a.m., or a bus to Puntarenas (Calle 12, Avenida 9), no later than 11 a.m. Better yet, avoid Puntarenas altogether, and take a bus from the Coca-Cola terminal in San José (16 Calle, Avenidas 1/3), heading toward Cañas, Liberia or Peñas Blancas. Leave no later than 11:30 a.m., and ask to be let off at the Lagarto junction, at kilometer post 149. The Monteverde bus passes this junction at about 3 p.m.

From the junction, it's a two-hour ascent on a bumpy, unpaved road to Santa Elena, with spectacular views, on a clear evening, of the sunset and orange-tinged sky over the Nicoya Peninsula, below and in the distance. When visibility is limited, you'll have to settle for views of the nearby landscape, as it changes from rolling hills covered with citrus and mango trees to steep grazing lands on the slopes of the mountain ridge, patches of oak and evergreen forest, and many a cool, misty valley with scattered clusters of farmhouses.

By automobile, follow the Pan American Highway (Route 1) to the junction at kilometer 149, then the dirt road for 32

126

kilometers to Santa Elena. This last stretch will usually take at least an hour and a half to cover.

Most travel agencies in San José offer tours to Monteverde. Transportation can be arranged as well through some of the hotels mentioned below.

Accommodations

Santa Elena is a pleasant little town, about 1500 meters above sea level, though the dramatic, broken landscape all around, the strong winds, and the cool, misty air make it seem higher. There are numerous bars, and also a few lodging places. A room in the pleasant and simple Pensión Santa Elena costs less than $3 per person. Other establishments charge about the same.

However, if you have the energy to walk after you arrive, probably in the evening, you might as well stay nearer to the reserve. The pensions and hotel mentioned below are located from two to three kilometers uphill from Santa Elena, along or near the road to the reserve. You may be able to pick up a ride from locals, who charge about a dollar for the service. Bear in mind that you'll face an early start on the day you leave to catch the 6 a.m. bus down from Santa Elena. Traffic is sparse, so don't count on being able to hitch a ride at a later hour.

Hotel de Montaña Monteverde, 12 rooms, $38 to $70 double, meals additional. Tel. 611846. San José address: P. O. Box 70, tel. 333890. U.S. reservations: tel. 800-327-4250.

Located on the east side of the road to the reserve, about two kilometers from Santa Elena, the Hotel de Montaña is cozy and rustic, with hardwood-panelled rooms, and beds covered with thick woolen blankets. Food is quite good, with an emphasis on beef. There are acres of adjoining farm and woods available to guests for exploration, and spectacular views down toward the Pacific. Horses are available for rent, and boots are lent for hiking through the reserve. Transportation to the hotel may be arranged through the San José telephone number.

Pensión Quetzal, 8 rooms. $19 per person with three meals. Tel. 611929.

This is a comfortable lodge with a homey atmosphere, also heavy on the wood panelling, located about half a kilometer beyond the Hotel de Montaña, and 150 meters back from the road. The food is good.

Camparque

Half a kilometer past the turn for Pensión Quetzal, this campsite, with its tin-roofed shelter, has seen better days. Inquire at the Pensión Flor Mar if you wish to stay here.

Pensión Flor Mar, 6 rooms. $11 per person with three meals. Telephone 611887.

Three kilometers from Santa Elena and three from the reserve, the Flor Mar is a rustic place that reminds me of a summer camp. Basic, friendly and American-run. You sleep on bunks, and can have a room all to yourself if they're not too busy. The food is vegetarian and hearty, and they'll pack a lunch to carry to the reserve if you so desire. This is probably the only place in Costa Rica that serves imitation coffee.

Meals without lodging are available at the Hotel de Montaña and the Pensión Flor Mar, and at a couple of diners in Santa Elena.

Visiting the Reserve

The Monteverde cloud forest is created by winds, temperature, moisture conditions, and mountainous topography, which combine during the dry season to hold a steady cloud cover along the continental divide, where Monteverde is situated. During the rainy season, of course, the forest receives its full share of precipitation from storms blowing up from the coast. The rains, and the moisture in the air, nourish trees and plants rooted in the ground, as well as many plants that live at the upper levels of the forest, and take their nutrients directly from the mist and dust that pass through the air around them. The result is an enchanted, fairy-tale environment, where trees are laden with orchids, bromeliads, mosses and ferns that obscure their branches, where the moisture and mild temperatures and sunlight filtered by the forest canopy encourage the exuberance of begonias, heliconias, philodendron and many other tropical plants in every

128

available space on the ground. Leaves are gigantic, vines penetrate everywhere, flowers blow through the air from the tree canopy. The forest is almost visibly growing and changing, throbbing and vibrating with life at all levels. Hummingbirds feed on nectar, frogs use pools of rainwater trapped in bromeliads to rear their young, worms and tree roots alike mine decaying matter whether it lies on the ground or in the crook of a branch. The air resounds with a crack as an epiphyte-laden branch drops to the ground, to rot and return to life by feeding the creatures and plants all around.

More than 2000 plant species have been catalogued at Monteverde. Within the 2500-hectare reserve there is a variety in the forest habitat. Parts are relatively dry, with little under-growth, others are swampy. There are areas of dwarf trees, and gradations from premontane to rain and cloud forest.

And, of course, there is more to the forest than the trees and lesser plants. Of over 320 bird species, the most notable is the quetzal, with its long arc of tail feathers. It nests in the trunks of dead trees. Other trogons inhabit the reserve as well, along with more than 50 varieties of hummingbird. Among the more than 100 mammalian species are howler, white-faced and spider monkeys, coatis and their cousins, raccoons; and pumas, ocelots, jaguars, tapirs, kinkajous, and, of course, the golden toad, a symbol of the natural treasures that may turn up in protected areas. Some of these may be seen scurrying for cover as you walk through their territory.

There are no specific hours for visiting the Monteverde Reserve. Go as early or late as you like, sign in, and pay your entry fee of about $2. Give the person at the reception desk an idea of your route so that somebody may look for you if you don't return. On sale at the entrance are bird and plant lists, as well as a guide for the nature trail (which is marked only with numbers).

Camping is permitted near the entrance for a small fee. There are, as well, two cabins well inside the reserve, available for rent. Take along supplies if you would like to use these.

Trails are well marked, and it would be difficult to lose your way. There is some mud (more squishy leaf rot than shoe-sucking ooze) and damp terrain, but thoughtful planners have placed plank bridges and stump steps wherever they are needed. Leon

Bean's Maine hunting shoe would be the ideal footwear for a walk in these woods, but otherwise, any sturdy walking shoe and an eye to where you step are all that are needed. Elevations vary from about 1500 to 1700 meters. Most of the steeper grades are near the entrance, so don't be discouraged. You'll be handed a map when you pay your fee. Any of several routes are possible, for walks of a few hours to a few days. While you're supposed to come to look at the forest and animals, the long-distance views are also magnificent, especially from the point called La Ventana (The Window, or Opening). However, you will be very lucky indeed if you see an ocean. This is, after all, a cloud forest, and the clouds are often there.

One last bit of advice before you take off on your walk is to go slowly. Stop every once in a while and take a 360-degree look around at the moss- and bromeliad-laden canopy, and at the lower levels of the forest. If you only walk at a steady pace— in other words, if you hike—your eyes will be necessarily glued to the trail in order to keep your footing, and you'll miss the whole show overhead.

Those planning an intensive acquaintance with the reserve can pick up pamphlets about its wildlife (in English and Spanish) at the Tropical Science Center, Calle 1, Avenidas 2/4 (No. 442), San José, telephone 226241.

Aside from the reserve, the only site to see in Monteverde is the cheese factory. Visitors may look through a window at the operations inside, which are unspectacular.

The Monteverde community as a whole attracts much curiosity. It is, after all, unusual to find an English-speaking, North American farming colony dispersed over these beautiful mountains. Outsiders are treated courteously, but the local residents would just as well be left to their labors.

From Monteverde, one can descend again to the main highway, and continue by bus or car to the northwest. At kilometer 168 is the junction for a road that goes to the town of Nicoya and the Nicoya peninsula, via a ferry crossing of the Tempisque River. Along the way is Barra Honda National Park, with its many caves (mentioned below).

At kilometer 188 is the farming center of Cañas. From here,

130

a branch road leads 40 kilometers back into the mountains to the Arenal Dam, Costa Rica's newest hydroelectric project. Lake Arenal is said to be good for sport fishing; guapote, a bass-like fish, and machaca populate its waters. There is frequent bus service from Cañas to Tilarán, at the base of the mountains. A few buses a day go up to the lake and to the town of Arenal. Poor roads continue along the northern side of the ridge to Fortuna and Ciudad Quesada (San Carlos), on the San Carlos plain. Mount Arenal (1633 meters), which overlooks the area, has the distinction of being the volcano in Costa Rica that most *looks* like a volcano, with a distinctive cone shape. It also acts like one, having erupted spectacularly in 1968 and spewed ashes over a wide area. The glow of the active crater may often be seen at night. Arenal is considered too hot and dangerous to climb.

Southwest of Cañas, near the mouth of the Tempisque River, is Palo Verde National Park, a reserve of seasonally dry tropical forest, which once covered much of this area. Adjacent is a wetland wildlife refuge frequented by migrating waterfowl. No services are available at the park, and permission is required from the National Parks Service in San José before visiting. A separate permit from the Wildlife Department (Departmento de Vida Silvestre) of the Ministry of Agriculture is required to visit the wildlife refuge. Telephone 219533 for information.

LIBERIA

Population: 16,500; Altitude: 150 meters (492 feet); 236 kilometers from San José.

Liberia, the major city of northwestern Costa Rica, is a bustling place with wide, clean streets, relatively good accommodations, and a pleasant, dry climate. All lowland towns should be like Liberia. Strangely, this modern town has one of the relatively few surviving colonial churches, La Agonía. But this dates from a period when the area was part of Nicaragua, then a more prosperous and populated colony than Costa Rica.

Liberia is the capital of Guanacaste, a province with a separate tradition and a separate history from the rest of Costa Rica. By Spanish fiat, the area was detached from Nicaragua in 1814 in order to give Costa Rica a population sufficient for representation in the Cortes at Cadiz. A vote in Nicoya in 1820 confirmed the transfer, at a time when Nicaragua was racked by civil wars. That early exercise in self-determination is celebrated on July 25. Nicaragua for many years protested the loss of the territory, but finally gave up its claims in the Cañas-Jérez treaty of 1858.

The province takes its name from the guanacaste (earpod) tree that provides shade on vast, flat grasslands. In a country short on folklore, Guanacaste fills the role of providing tradition and color for all of Costa Rica. The punto guanacasteco is the national dance. Music played on the marimba, a xylophone-type instrument used by pre-Columbian Indians of Guanacaste, with sounding boxes made from wood or gourds, arouses nostalgic feelings in San José, though it has no roots there.

The culture of Guanacaste is largely Mestizo, or mixed Indian and Spanish. The Chorotega Indians of this area had strong ties to the peoples to the north, in Mexico and coastal Central America, before the arrival of the Spanish. Even today, there are pockets of Chorotega life in the Nicoya peninsula, where old farming practices, such as the use of the digging stick, and traditional forms of burnished pottery are maintained. Mostly, however, the Chorotega heritage may be seen in Guanacastecan faces that are browner than those in other parts of Costa Rica.

Large areas of drought-prone Guanacaste have been made productive for rice and cotton cultivation with the construction of irrigation systems. A sparse population produces surpluses of fruit, corn and beans as well. But for most Costa Ricans, Guanacaste signifies vast herds of cattle munching away on the grasslands. The folkloric figures par excellence of the area are Costa Rica's poor man's cowboys, mounted on horses with elaborately decorated saddles, and boyeros, tenders of oxen.

Accommodations

Hotel El Bramadero, tel. 660203. 22 rooms, $10 single/$15 double.

A modest motel with rooms arranged around a courtyard. Air-conditioned, but no hot water. Swimming pool sometimes filled. The large pavilion restaurant is fairly good, specializing in beef,

132

as do most eateries in this area. Located at the turn from the highway into town.

Nuevo Hotel Boyeros, tel. 660722. 62 rooms. **$16/$25.**

Also located at the turn into town. Modern, with air conditioning and a pool. Unfortunately, this hotel is a local social center, and a loud band sometimes performs late into the night.

Hotel La Siesta, Calle 4, Avenidas 4/6, tel. 660678, 25 rooms, $12/$20.

Nice hotel, with pool and air conditioning, nearest to the bus station (from the Central Park, walk one block toward the highway on Avenida Central, then two blocks to the left).

Hotel Las Espuelas, tel. 660144. 39 rooms. **$25/$34.**

Best in the area, with a good restaurant, air conditioning and pool. Located on the highway, about a kilometer south of the turn into town.

Hotel La Ronda, tel. 660417. 21 rooms. $12/$20.

Located on the highway near the above hotel. Pool and air conditioning, modest rooms.

All of the above have restaurants and bars. In addition, a few Chinese restaurants in the downtown area—the Cuatro Mares, the Hong Kong and the Kam Puy—serve reasonably priced meals.

Transportation

Liberia is the crossroads of northwestern Costa Rica. Buses leave here for the main towns of the Nicoya Peninsula, the Nicaraguan border, and several beaches.

Buses for Liberia leave from 14 Calle, Avenidas 1/3, San José, every day at 7, 9, and 11:30 a.m., and 1, 4, 6 and 8 p.m. Most are modern units, and cover the route in about four hours. There are additional buses from the Coca-Cola station in San José serving Peñas Blancas on the Nicaraguan border, and Playa El Coco via Liberia.

From the terminal in Liberia, next to the square, buses leave for Peñas Blancas and the border of Nicaragua approximately every two hours, starting at 8:30 a.m. These buses will drop you on the road to Santa Rosa National Park. Buses for El Coco beach leave at 5:30 a.m., 12:30 p.m. and 4:30 p.m. At 11:30 a.m., there's a bus to Playa Hermosa. Slow buses to Santa Cruz and Nicoya leave every one to two hours throughout the day.

SANSA, the domestic airline, currently has flights from San José to Liberia, via Tamarindo Beach, on Mondays, Wednesdays and Fridays, departing at noon. The direct return flight leaves Liberia at 1:35 p.m. The airport is located about 10 kilometers from Liberia on the road to Nicoya.

RINCON DE LA VIEJA NATIONAL PARK

The Rincón de la Vieja volcano, one of five in the Guanacaste range, lies northeast of Liberia, and rises to an altitude of 1895 meters (6216 feet). Slopes steaming with mud pots, hot springs and geysers; heavy rainfall and resultant lush vegetation; abundant mammalian wildlife (white-faced monkeys, collared peccaries, and especially coatimundis); and a variety of birds all create a rare combination of sights and experiences for the visitor to the volcano and the surrounding forest.

The ascent of Rincón de la Vieja is completed in two stages. First comes a walk of two to three hours from park headquarters to the Las Pailas area, where mud bubbles and shoots into the air. From there, the climb to the summit takes six to seven hours. Severe winds, suddenly dropping temperatures, fog, rain, and loose, rocky volcanic debris underfoot can make the going difficult and the rewards elusive. A morning ascent during the driest months (December to May) is recommended for the best views at the summit. But even if the peak is obscured, the clouds may blow away if you sit and wait.

A permit is required for a visit to Rincón de la Vieja National Park. You can drive via Colonia La Libertad to the park entrance, 27 kilometers from Liberia. Or, the park service may help you get a ride on the milk truck that passes the entrance. It leaves from the general store (pulpería) called La Casita in the Victoria neighborhood of Liberia (tel. 661174). There are also occasional buses from Liberia for Colonia La Libertad that pass the park entrance, a half-hour walk from the administration area. Inquire at the bus terminal in Liberia.

Camping in the park is permitted, and is recommended in order to get an early start toward the summit from the mudpot area.

SANTA ROSA NATIONAL PARK

Located 36 kilometers north of Liberia, Santa Rosa National Park was established in 1971 as a historical monument. The natural treasures of the park, which were originally included only incidentally, are now the main attraction for the foreign visitor.

The Santa Rosa hacienda was the scene of one of Costa Rica's most glorious military episodes—an episode that lasted the approximately fourteen minutes it took for a Costa Rican force to defeat the invading army of William Walker on March 20, 1856. Walker's army—and much of the opposing Costa Rican army as well—was finished off not long afterward in a cholera epidemic. The original great house of the Santa Rosa hacienda still stands as a monument to the Costa Rican victory. Santa Rosa's location near the Nicaraguan border made it the scene of later intrigues and battles as well, most notably during a 1955 invasion by political exiles.

Among the many natural features of the park are the only protected area of deciduous dry tropical forest from Mexico to Colombia; and Nancite beach, where hundreds of thousands of Pacific Ridley turtles nest from August until December every year.

Visiting Santa Rosa

The main facilities of the park are eight kilometers west of the Pan American Highway. Buses leave Liberia for La Cruz every hour or so during the day, passing the junction for the park. From San José, buses of the Tralapa company depart from Avenida 3, Calle 16, at 4:45 a.m., 7:45 a.m. and 4:15 p.m. Time to the junction is about four hours. Telephone 217202 to confirm schedules. There are other buses as well from the area of the Coca-Cola terminal. If you're not driving, you'll have to hitch or, more likely, walk from the highway to the hacienda building and administration center.

Facilities at or near the park center include a historical museum in the old great house of the hacienda; a campsite with showers, and a nature trail. Partly because of its historical importance, the park is quite well run, and is one of the most visited in the national park system. Best time to visit Santa Rosa is in the dry season, when thirsty animals congregate around the permanent waterholes and streams, making for easy viewing.

The casona, or great house of the Santa Rosa hacienda, is a large whitewashed building with aged tile roof and wooden verandas. Part of the casona may date from the colonial period, though the age of the building is indeterminate. Houses of this sort were continually repaired, remodeled and expanded during their useful lives. The stone corrals around the house are almost certainly a few hundred years old, and were in use until the hacienda was nationalized.

Along the kilometer-long nature trail, signs point out features of plants, such as seasonal loss of leaves, which are adapted to the scarcity of water for much of the year; rock formations; and plants that survive the periodic fires of the dry lands. Typical dry-forest vegetation includes oaks, wild cherry, mahogany and the calabash, or gourd tree, the acacia bush, the ficus or *amate* tree and the gumbo limbo, also called the naked Indian from the rich, reddish-brown color of its bark.

At the waterholes in the park, during the dry season, one can sit at a prudent and non-interfering distance and watch raccoons, coatis, spider monkeys, tapirs, agoutis, deer and assorted birds take their turns at the trough. Other wildlife that is more or less easily spotted in the dry season includes white-faced and howler monkeys, ocelots, jaguars, coyotes, armadillos, iguanas, collared and white-lipped peccaries, and rabbits. As well, more than 250 bird species have been recorded.

Much of the savanna of the central part of Santa Rosa was created through clearing of the native forest. The grass periodically burns off, either through accidental fires or controlled fires set by park personnel. Efforts are being made to regenerate the forest in these areas. Typically for Costa Rica, there are several habitats in the park beside seasonally dry forest. Moister areas contain abundant hardwoods that never lose their leaves. Gallery forest sweeps over the park's waterways. Near the coast are man-

136

grove swamps, with dense populations of crabs, and high, sandy beach.

Nancite beach is one of two known nesting areas in Central America for the Pacific Ridley sea turtle. During the rainy season, the turtles crawl up onto the beach, first by the dozens, then the hundreds, then the thousands, to shove each other aside like so many commuters fighting for space, dig nests, and lay eggs before departing for the open sea. Green and leatherback turtles nest at the beach as well, but in smaller numbers than the Ridleys. With humans and other predators scooping up the eggs when park employees aren't looking, and vultures and frigate birds diving down for bits of hatchlings, less than one percent of the eggs make it to the sea as young turtles. Crabs and sharks lie in wait to further deplete their numbers.

Naranjo, a larger beach than Nancite, is an excellent locale for bird watching. Cuajiniquil Canyon, at the northern edge of the park, contains a series of waterfalls, as well as numerous palms and ferns in its moist environment. Platanar Lake, covering a hectare, is four kilometers north of the great house and administrative area, and attracts varied waterfowl as well as mammals during the dry season.

North of the main section of Santa Rosa Park is the Murciélago addition, a rugged, seaside strip of scrub forest and rocky outcrops where jaguars and mountain lions roam. The park land was expropriated by the Costa Rican government from former Nicaraguan president Anastasio Somoza. Access is via the Pan American Highway to Cuajiniquil, the turnoff for which is 30 kilometers north of the junction for the main section of Santa Rosa Park. The Murciélago addition entrance is eight kilometers from Cuajiniquil. Buses operate once a day at noon from La Cruz, 20 kilometers from the Nicaraguan border on the Pan American Highway, to Cuajiniquil. No facilities for visitors are provided.

Peñas Blancas, 311 kilometers (194 miles) from San José on the Pan American Highway, is the small town located on the border with Nicaragua. If you plan to visit Nicaragua, it's advisable to first obtain a visa in San José. Latest currency regulations in Nicaragua call for visitors to exchange $60 at the official rate when entering. Nicaraguan currency is available at a substantial discount at some banks in San José.

The border is open from 6:30 a.m. to 11 a.m., 12:30 p.m. to 5:30 p.m., and 6:30 p.m. to 10 p.m. Buses operate between Peñas Blancas and Liberia approximately every two hours, and there are several buses a day to San José.

THE NICOYA PENINSULA

The Nicoya Peninsula is separated from the rest of Costa Rica by the Gulf of Nicoya, as well as by its Indian heritage and colonial history as a part of Nicaragua. Sparsely populated, with poor roads, Nicoya enjoys a relatively dry climate, due to the barrier of hills and low mountains along the coast. Those same mountains create a series of sun-drenched beaches with rugged, dramatic backdrops (more on these later). Inland are some of the oldest towns in Costa Rica, as well as the mountain-trimmed plains where cowboys rope stray horses and calves (often right on the road you're trying to negotiate), and fields of sorghum, sugarcane and irrigated rice ripen in the sun. In parts of Nicoya, as in few other areas of Costa Rica, steep hillside plots of corn are laboriously cultivated with hand tools, using methods that have not changed in hundreds of years.

There are several routes into Nicoya: by ferry from Puntarenas to Playa Naranjo or Paquera; by the road that branches from the Pan American Highway at kilometer 168, with a ferry crossing at the Tempisque River; and by the main highway south from Liberia to Santa Cruz and the town of Nicoya.

Santa Cruz (population approximately 6000, 56 kilometers from Liberia) is a sleepy, clean, pleasant, sunny and hot town, with a ruinous bell tower surviving from a colonial church. Several stores here sell pottery made in Nicoya's particular style, brown-colored and often with tripod bases, much of it made by Chorotega Indians in Guaitil, a craft center near Santa Barbara, about ten kilometers to the east.

For most visitors, Santa Cruz is a stopping point on the way to some of the Pacific beaches. The Marbella bus leaves at 10:30 a.m. for Tamarindo, arriving at 12:10 p.m. and turning around immediately. Phone 680145 to confirm the schedule. The Costa

Mar bus for Junquillal beach leaves at 11:30 a.m.

The two main hotels are the Diriá (28 rooms, tel. 680080, $14 single, $20 double), a roadside establishment on the edge of town, with plain, air-conditioned rooms and a pool; and the Sharatoga (39 rooms, tel. 680011, or 336664 in San José, $14 single, $18 double), located a few blocks in from the highway, also with air conditioning, and harsh, bare rooms. Either place is acceptable for spending a night on the way through. Also in Santa Cruz are several Chinese restaurants, those saviors of the traveler's stomach in Costa Rica.

Nicoya (population approximately 10,000), the major town in the peninsula, is another 22 kilometers down the road from Santa Cruz. A commercial and cattle center, its single point of interest is an attractive, whitewashed, tin-roofed colonial church, one of the oldest in Costa Rica.

Places to stay in Nicoya include the plain and adequate Hotel Las Tinajas (tel. 685081, $6 single, $9 double), located next to the terminal for buses to the beaches; and the Chorotega (tel. 685245, $3 per person), two blocks south of the square, clean and a good value. The pleasant Hotel Curimé, a few kilometers south of town (tel. 685238), has 20 bungalows, each with twin beds, that go for about $45 per night. Several Chinese restaurants on the square serve good meals for $3 to $4.

Buses leave for Nicoya from the Coca-Cola terminal, Calle 16, Avenidas 1/3, San José, at 6:30 a.m., 10 a.m., 1:30 p.m., 3 p.m. and 5 p.m. Empresa Rojas (tel. 685352) operates buses from Nicoya to Playa Naranjo at 5 a.m. and 1 p.m., meeting the ferry for Puntarenas; to Nosara beach at noon; and to Sámara and Carrillo beaches at 3 p.m.

About 14 kilometers northeast of Nicoya, off the road that leads to the Tempisque River and the Pan American Highway, is Barra Honda National Park, with its extensive limestone caverns, and peaks offering long-distance views out over the Gulf of Nicoya.

Barra Honda mountain, once thought to be a volcano, rises 300 meters above the surrounding plain, and is pocked by holes where the roofs of underlying caves have collapsed. The caves were formed—and are still being formed—by the rapid erosion and chemical decomposition of layers of limestone sediment that once lay on the bed of a prehistoric sea. A geological fault line runs roughly along the nearby Tempisque River, and the former seabed was steadily lifted as the Nicoya Peninsula slid alongside the mainland.

There are more than two dozen caves in Barra Honda, some of them still unexplored. Most are entered by vertical drops, and the difficulty of entrance may account for their excellent state of preservation. Various caves have stalactites, stalagmites, soda straws, cave grapes, popcorn, fried eggs, and numerous other formations. Pozo Hediondo, once thought to be a crater, reeks with bat guano, though the bat population of the other caves is low. Other denizens of the dark are rats, insects, birds and blind fish. Nicoa cave contains skeletal human remains, some grotesquely meshed with stalagmates or covered with layers of calcium carbonate.

No facilities are provided at Barra Honda Park other than trails and drinking water. The park headquarters are in the town of Barra Honda, four kilometers west of the highway at Quebrada Honda. Alfaro buses from San José to the town of Hojancha pass the turn for Barra Honda after dark. More feasibly, travel first to the town of Nicoya, then take a morning bus heading by Quebrada Honda. Advance notice to the National Park Service in San José is required before visiting the park.

East from the town of Nicoya, the main highway runs for 75 kilometers (the last 40 unpaved) to the ferry slip at Playa Naranjo, through sugarcane fields, and pastures broken by clumps of trees, and bordered by windbreaks. The plain is edged by mountains, but at a few high spots along the way, tantalizing glimpses of the Gulf of Nicoya are available. The distance is covered in four hours by slow (and dusty) bus, in half that time by car.

BEACHES, BEACHES, BEACHES

First, the good news. Along the coast of Nicoya Peninsula are dozens of beaches, each set in its own sweep of bay, bordered by rocky promontories and hills and coconut palms and lush

140

tropical foliage, drenched in sun, with views to glittering blue sea broken here and there by huge rocks and by islets. Some of the beaches are virtually deserted, others have luxury hotels where most of one's needs are anticipated and attended. Commerical exploitation is limited. There are no coral jewelry salesmen to hound sunbathers, nor noisy discos, nor beachwear shops, and rarely are there crowds.

Now, the bad news (or hard facts). The nicest beaches in Nicoya are difficult to reach. Most of the roads to the coast are dusty and rutted, or muddy and occasionally impassable, depending on the time of year. Buses reach most of the coastal villages only once a day, after crunching, thumping, seemingly interminable (but only 30-kilometer-long) rides and numerous river fordings from Santa Cruz or Nicoya, and deliver passengers with a new coat of fine, reddish-brown grit. A few beaches are served by bus with less than daily frequency, and some not at all. Getting from one beach to another is often difficult, if not impossible. The motto of public transportation in Nicoya might as well be "you can't get there from here." The alternative to bus travel is to rent a car (an expensive proposition in Costa Rica), and brave the roads on your own. If you can find your way, that is. Some roads shown on maps of Nicoya exist only in the minds of hopeful cartographers.

Beyond the problems of getting to them, Costa Rica's Pacific beaches have far fewer facilities than one might expect from the publicity about them. There are only a few hundred first-class rooms in the hundreds of kilometers of coastline from the Nicaraguan border to Panama. Most of the remaining accommodations are "cabinas," budget-priced rooms with cold water only. There is no middle range.

Restaurants at the beaches are few and offer little variety, while food at the hotels—with some exceptions—is not what one expects at a resort. There is little opportunity for shopping and browsing, nor are there car-rental agencies, dive shops, or many of the amenities one associates with a beach resort. Food stocks in stores—where there are stores—are limited to a few basics.

But the bad news may also be good news. So many of the Nicoya beaches are nearly deserted and unspoiled precisely because they are hard to reach. If your intention really is to swim and take the sun and read and enjoy some special company

141

without any distractions, then there are few better places to go than the less accessible beaches of Nicoya. As overnight destinations during a week of hopping around Costa Rica, forget them But for a few days at a time at least, most are fairly wonderful.

To make your beach excursion easier, consider renting a car, even if you normally use public transportation. Fill up on gas at every opportunity—filling stations are sparse. Or else hire a taxi to take you, say, from the town of Nicoya or Santa Cruz to one of the beaches. This will cost $20 or so—not excessive for two people or more—and save much time as well as personal wear and tear. Some beach hotels and travel agencies will also make transportation arrangements. Call ahead, when you can, to reserve a room and to allow your hosts to lay in supplies—a difficult task at beaches. Reconfirm bus departure times. If you're backpacking and camping out—tempting on deserted stretches of coast—take supplies from San José or some other large town. If there are children in your group, take a variety of snacks (a good idea for adults, too). And take a supply of cash—you won't find any banks to exchange travelers checks. In general, don't count on finding anything out there that you haven't been told is there.

Here's a rundown of some of the beach resorts on the Nicoya coast, from north to south.

PLAYA HERMOSA

This is one of the easiest beaches to reach from San José by road, and it has been targeted with ambitious development plans. For the present, though, Playa Hermosa is more serene than Playa El Coco, just to the south. The beach is reached by a daily 11:30 a.m. bus from Liberia, about 35 kilometers away. To drive to Playa Hermosa or Playa del Coco, take the main Nicoya highway from Liberia and turn off at the Tamarindo restaurant.

Condovac La Costa, tel. 680474. 100 units, $70 single/$80 double.

U. S. Reservations: 800-327-9408, 305-588-8541.

Condovac is a vacation village with individual cottages arranged in camp-style rows on a hillside. Amenities include water skiing and fishing facilities, sailing, a nice sandy beach, Spanish-style dining room, pool, air conditioning, tennis. Each unit has a bedroom, kitchenette, bathroom and living room with convertible sofa. A small store sells groceries. These are time-sharing units, and are sometimes advertised in San José newspapers at discounted rates.

More modest accommodations are available at the Hotel Playa Hermosa and several cabinas.

PLAYAS DEL COCO

The beach here is in a dramatic setting on a large bay with great rocks offshore, and sailboats gliding around. The little town and the central part of the beach are dirty, but there's less litter the farther you walk from the highway. Buses leave Liberia for Coco, about 32 kilometers away, at 5:30 a.m., 12:30 p.m. and 4:30 p.m., from Coco for Liberia at 7 a.m., 2 p.m. and 6 p.m. One bus a day leaves from the Coca-Cola terminal in San José at 10 a.m. for El Coco, and there's a departure for San José at 9:15 a.m. Coco is about four kilometers south of Playa Hermosa.

The Hotel Casino Playas del Coco (tel. 670110) offers cabina-type rooms with sea view and private bath for $7 single, $9 double. If you're stuck in back, the rate is about a dollar lower. Boat rentals are available here. Similar quarters are available at Cabinas Luna Tica.

PLAYA OCOTAL

Three kilometers south of El Coco, Ocotal is the site of a miniscule and exclusive resort.

Hotel El Ocotal, tel 660166. 6 cottages. $100 double.

San José address: P. O. Box 1013, tel. 224259.

The luxurious cottages here are in a bare but dramatic clifftop setting overlooking a black sand beach. Facilities include tennis courts, pool, riding horses, and equipment for fishing, water skiing and scuba diving. Deep-sea fishing programs, using 20- and 30-foot boats, are available at $200 to $250 per person per day, including all meals.

PLAYA TAMARINDO

Tamarindo is a wide, mostly empty beach curving around a miles-long bay, with rocks and little sandy islands offshore. Pelicans float overhead and dive into the waters, skiffs bob up and down in the gentle surf. There is no real village, only a few houses spread out along the last stretch of road, and a couple of hotels. The setting is nearly perfect. And yet, many who know the Nicoya beaches say that Tamarindo is spoiled. Which is a measure of what some of the other beaches are like.

Hotel Tamarindo Diriá, tel. 680474. 60 rooms. $57 single/$65 double. San José office: P. O. Box 4211, tel 330530.

A pleasant motel with nicely furnished rooms in Spanish-colonial style, lovely landscaped grounds, and a pool. Air conditioned. Water skiing and fishing are available.

Cabinas Zullymar. $7 per person. Tel. 264732.

At the end of the road, cold-water rooms with private bath. The owner is weird but nice. Across the road from the Zullymar is its Bar El Tercer Mundo (Third-World Bar), worth a visit for the name alone. Good, plain food is served, mostly beef and fish, for $3 to $4 per entree.

The road from Santa Cruz to Tamarindo is typically potholed. The Marbella bus (tel. 680145) leaves Santa Cruz at 10:30 a.m. for Tamarindo, arrives just after noon, and departs immediately for Santa Cruz. There is air service as well, on SANSA airlines. Flights leave San José Monday, Wednesday and Friday at noon, arrive in Tamarindo at 12:40 p.m., and continue to Liberia and back to San José.

144

PLAYA JUNQUILLAL

Nobody lives here but three native families and the resident foreigners who own all the hotels. The beach is empty, clean and beautiful, on a two-kilometer-wide bay trimmed by rocky out-crops at either end. Like a number of other Nicoya beaches, Junquillal is a favorite nesting site for sea turtles during the rainy season.

Hotel Antumalal, tel. 680506. 20 cottages, $80 single/$100 double with meals.

A tasteful cluster of colonial-style buildings on a hill overlook-ing the sea. Pool with bar, tennis court, lovely thatched dining pavilion. Friendly management. The food is some of the best on the coast. Located about 500 meters down the beach from the other hotels.

Villa Serena, tel 680737. 4 rooms. $80 per couple with meals.

Not on the beach, but an intimate little estate, with large, com-fortable rooms. Facilities include a video cassette player and library, riding horses, sauna and game room. All rooms have terraces facing the ocean. Children not allowed. Nice for getting away from it all.

Tortuga Inn, $12 per person with three meals.

You share a small primitive house here with an American and his Costa Rican wife. Friendly, a few yards from the beach.

Hotel Playa Junquillal, $12 per person.

Basic, modest cubicles.

The Costa Mar bus (tel. 680145) leaves Santa Cruz most days at 11:30 a.m. for Junquillal, arrives at about 2 p.m., and turns around. Another bus leaves Santa Cruz at 2:30 p.m. for Paraíso, four kilometers from Junquillal, and departs for Santa Cruz the next morning at 5:45 a.m.

PLAYA NOSARA

Nosara is the favorite of retired foreigners who have settled down to life by the sea. It's not that the beach here is superior to those elsewhere on the peninsula (although it's nice), only that hustlers of building lots staked out land here first and did a better job of selling in San José. Land sales to foreigners constitute one of the more visible economic activities in parts of Nicoya, and the visitor to Costa Rica is sure to come across some compatriot who is harvesting basketsful of cash at least in his dreams in the land business. (There are also the coconut business, the mango business, the shrimp business, the jojoba business and others in which your buddies from home will deal you in on "secure" future profits for a substantial investment now, but those are other stories.) Various hotels in Nicoya exist at least partly to encourage the romance between visitor and house lot. There is no reason to get a creepy feeling about real estate activities in Nosara or elsewhere—the climate, the views and much else are attractive. But one should bear in mind that promised amenities, such as electricity, running water, transportation and shopping, may not materialize during your lifetime.

Hotel Playa Nosara, tel. 680495. 8 rooms. $25 single/$35 double.

Air-conditioned rooms, bar, restaurant.

Nosara is reached by a poor dirt road from the town of Nicoya. Empresa Rojas (tel. 685352) buses run once a day from Nicoya at noon.

SAMARA AND CARRILLO

Both of these beaches have more modest accommodations than Nosara, in cabinas. At Sámara, Turicentro Don Tino (tel. 680445) offers rooms for about $5 per person, and has a basic restaurant and bar. In Carrillo, the Hotel Playa Hermosa (tel. 660366, ext. 110) has similar modest rooms for slightly higher prices. There are other simple lodging places at both beaches. Access is by a dirt road from Nicoya, about 40 kilometers away.

Empresa Rojas buses leave Nicoya for Sámara and Carrillo at noon.

At the very end of the Nicoya Peninsula are the Cabo Blanco reserve and the beaches of Montezuma and Tambor, all reached most easily by ferry from Puntarenas.

CABO BLANCO ABSOLUTE NATURE RESERVE

Located at the southeastern point of the Nicoya Peninsula, the Cabo Blanco reserve is not as absolute as its name implies. Visitors are allowed in to watch the birds (especially pelicans, frigate birds and various others that frequent the shore), as well as howler monkeys, porcupines, abundant crabs, and the creatures that become trapped in tidal pools. The woods here in the rainiest part of Nicoya are classified as moist tropical forest, and have many more evergreens than those in the northern part of the peninsula. The shoreline is rocky, and beaches are therefore few and small. Off the very tip is Cabo Blanco island, a rock that is white with encrusted guano during the dry season.

Access to the reserve is only by car, and the park service in San José requests advance notification of any visit.

MONTEZUMA

Isolation and tranquility are features at this end-of-the-road beach, reached by car from Playa Naranjo, or taxi from Tambor. The little Hotel Montezuma (tel. 611122) is a pleasant stopping-point, with modest facilities and modest tariffs (about $6 per person).

TAMBOR

Tambor is another favorite place of retired foreigners, given its relative proximity to San José by car and ferry. Access is by car from Playa Naranjo, or bus from Paquera (where the passenger boat from Puntarenas lands). The attractive Hotel La Hacienda (tel. 612980) has 16 small rooms going for about $60 double. Apartments are also available for rent.

PLAYA NARANJO

There's no beach here, despite the name of the town ("Orange Tree Beach"). In fact, there's hardly a town at all, only a ferry slip. There are, however, very attractive accommodations at the Hotel Oasis del Pacífico, 500 meters down the road from the dock.

The ferry leaves Playa Naranjo for Puntarenas at 9 a.m. and 6 p.m. (and at 1 p.m. Friday through Sunday in the dry season). Sailings from Puntarenas are at 7 a.m. and 4 p.m. (and 11 a.m. on dry-season Fridays and weekends). Phone 611069 to check schedules. The crossing takes a little over an hour. Buses for Nicoya, 75 kilometers, four hours and various river fordings away, meet the ferry.

Hotel Oasis del Pacífico, tel. 611555. 37 rooms. $35 single/$45 double. Reservations: tel. 232453, San José; P. O. Box 200, Puntarenas.

This is a beautiful complex of air-conditioned cottages on lush, landscaped grounds, one of the nicest hotels in the Nicoya peninsula, as well as one of the most accessible. Extensive facilities include tennis courts, a pool, a wide stretch of private beach (unfortunately, it's pebbly), riding horses, and a large restaurant-bar. Views over the peaceful Gulf of Nicoya are magnificent, and management is quite friendly. Yachts are welcome, and non-guests may use all facilities for a daily charge of about $2. Rates drop to half the above in the rainy season.

There is one other place to stay in Playa Naranjo, a single room available for about $7 per night. Turn right from the ferry slip and ask for the house of the Belgian.

Other beaches are plentiful all around the rim of Nicoya, some with basic lodging, some accessible only by seasonably passable dirt roads, some uninhabited but for wild creatures. Go and find them!

148

South of Puntarenas

The beaches south of Puntarenas are every bit as inviting and pleasing to the eye as those along the Nicoya Peninsula, though they differ in character. Most are more open and sweeping and exposed, with fewer bordering outcrops of rocks. The farther south you go, the more humid and rainy is the climate, and the more lush and exuberant the vegetation that runs up to the sand. The mugginess is always relieved and attenuated, however, by breezes blowing off the water.

There is one fact about the southern beaches that is often not mentioned in polite company: they are dangerous for swimming. Large volumes of water flow toward shore across a deceptively smooth, broad front of waves, then recede in fast-flowing unpredictable streams. These rip currents drive bathers out to sea from waist-high waters, and cause drownings on a regular basis. Those who suddenly find themselves far from shore should swim across the current to escape its pull, then head on in. If you are not a good swimmer, you should stay quite close to shore.

Beach hotels are concentrated at Jacó and at Manuel Antonio (near Quepos), but there are numerous little-frequented beaches as well where cabinas and similar basic accommodations are available. You can poke around and explore for some of these paradisical hideaways if you decide to rent a car in San José. By bus, such meanderings would be more difficult. There is only infrequent service along the unpaved road south of Jacó, the humidity is uncomfortably high just inland from the coast, the lesser beaches would have to be reached by jaunts of a kilometer or two along side roads, and you'll find it difficult to move on if you don't like what you see (or the facilities that you don't see) at the water's edge.

Access to the south coast is easiest by bus or car from San José. From Puntarenas, one has to backtrack by car or train to Orotina, a junction point for the highway that goes to the coast via Atenas.

PLAYA JACO

Jacó is the nearest of the beach resorts to San José, three hours

149

away by public bus, less by car, or a half-hour hop by chartered plane. The sweep of bay here is quite attractive, but the beach is not well taken care of. There's an adequate number of rooms (unless you come on a holiday weekend) in hotels that are in some respects not always adequate.

Hotel Jacó Beach, tel. 611250. 150 rooms. $48 single/$59 double. Reservations: tel. 324811 (San José), 800-327-9408, 305-588-8541 (U.S.A.)

Large rooms with nice grounds, two swimming pools, air-conditioned rooms, tennis courts. Transportation arrangements may be made through the Hotel Irazú in San José.

Hotel Cocal, tel. 224622. 9 rooms. $28/$33.
Air-conditioned rooms, pool.

There are, as well, basic cabinas at about $6 per person, a supermarket, bakery, and take-out chicken shop.

South of Jacó, the bumpy road passes through mile after mile of what were once neatly laid-out banana plantations. These have now been supplanted by equally neat plantations of oil palms and clusters of precise two-story worker housing. All this order is near the town called—what else?—La Palma. Outside of the plantations, tropical exuberance and disorder are more evident. Brown rivers ooze through mangrove and mud flats, and are negotiated by narrow planked trestles. The broad- and shiny-leafed plants characteristic of the humid tropics grow to ferocious dimensions. Towns are littered and ramshackle, and are few and far between. Iguanas dart across the road, and snakes slither out of the bushes. Sweat lubricates everything. The landscape is fascinating to look at, but there are few attractive stopping places, except the Damas Caves, located between Parrita and Quepos.

QUEPOS

Population: approximately 6700; 144 kilometers from San José.

Once a banana shipping center, Quepos saw its fortunes decline with those of the plantations nearby. The town is now languid, squalid, rotting and garbage-strewn, with a dirty beach. Who would guess that the nicest beaches in Costa Rica are just over the ridge? Read on.

MANUEL ANTONIO NATIONAL PARK

Seven kilometers beyond Quepos are the perfect beaches of Manuel Antonio National Park, each an arc of sand curving around a bay strewn with islands of rock, and shaded by green bordering forests. All are backdropped by dramatic cliffs. Manuel Antonio beach is one of the few places in Costa Rica where unspoiled primary forest grows right to the high-tide mark, allowing visitors to bathe at times in the shade.

South Espadilla is the northernmost of the park's beaches, followed by calmer Manuel Antonio beach, offshore of which are some coral spots. Last is Puerto Escondido, access to which is made difficult by the bordering rocky promontory.

A nature trail runs near to the water's edge through the forest of Manuel Antonio. Some of the most frequently observed animals are marmosets—the smallest of Costa Rican monkeys—white-faced and howler monkeys, raccoons, cavies, opossums, and two- and three-toed sloths. Easily sighted seabirds include frigate birds, pelicans, terns and brown boobies.

Accommodations

While Manuel Antonio itself was rescued from developers, in 1972, a variety of facilities crowds the edge of the park and continues up the bordering ridge, making this the easiest national park at which to stay. In addition to the lodging places mentioned below, there are campsites available within the park.

Hotel La Mariposa, tel. 770355. 10 rooms, $110 single/$140 double. U. S. reservations: tel. 800-223-5077. Canada: 800-268-7044.

The Mariposa is one of the more tasteful hotels in Costa Rica, an intimate, luxury establishment built in Spanish-colonial style in a dramatic clifftop setting. Each bi-level unit has a separate

151

living room and bedroom, and deck with ocean view. Service is excellent. Three-and-a-half kilometers out of Quepos. Quite a descent to the beach if you don't have a car or bicycle.

Apartamentos y Cabinas Divisamar, tel. 770371. $25/$35. A little cottage colony with a pool, across from the Mariposa.

Nearby is El Colibrí (tel. 770432, P.O. Box 94), a private house where Gilles and Pierre offer bed and breakfast for $25 double.

Hotel Arboleda, tel. 770414 (351169 in San José). $25/$50. Twenty airy, sea-view cabins, five kilometers out of Quepos.

Apartotel Karahé, tel. 770170. 7 units, $38 daily. Housekeeping cottages for three, with good sea view, on the hillside just before the beach, seven kilometers from Quepos.

Starting where the paved road ends (and where the bus leaves off passengers), there is a series of cabinas, basic, cold-water units with no services. Those nearest the road go for $3 to $6 per unit, without regard to how many people cram into the two beds. The more substantial Cabinas Manuel Antonio, 200 meters farther along the beach, charge $12 for up to five persons in a room. The cabinas set back from it are quieter and charge only $3 per person. All the cabinas, spread among the palms, are close enough to each other that you can look them over before selecting one to settle into for a while. All are likely to be full or nearly full on weekends, and deserted on weekdays.

The variety of inexpensive accommodations at Manuel Antonio attracts a lively, mostly young crowd. Many of the visitors are foreigners on extended travels. The beach is known as a good place to hang out for a while, trade information, recoup, and re-group.

Of several eateries at Manuel Antonio, the best is the large, open-air Mar y Sombra, located where the paved road meets the beach. A whole fried fish goes for $3 to $4, depending on the size, and there are huge tropical fruit plates, as well as the usual beef dishes and sandwiches.

Transportation

Transportes Delio Morales buses depart from the Coca-Cola

terminal in San José (Calle 16, Avenidas 1/3) for Quepos at 7 a.m., 10 a.m., 2 p.m. and 4 p.m. The trip takes five hours, and can be nausea-inducing on the run down to the coast. Departures from Quepos are at 6 a.m., 7:30 a.m., 2 p.m. and 4 p.m. On weekends, it's best to buy your ticket in advance at the bus company office inside the Coca-Cola market.

A local bus for Manuel Antonio departs about every two hours from the bus stop in Quepos.

SANSA, the domestic airline, has two flights from San José to Quepos every day except Sunday, departing at 5:30 a.m. and 12:15 p.m. Return flights are at 6:10 a.m. and 12:55 p.m. On Sundays, departure from San José is at 10 a.m., from Quepos at 10:40 p.m. As on all domestic flights, fares are quite low—currently about $13 one way.

About 50 kilometers south of Quepos on a poor road is Dominical, a beautiful beach with basic accommodations. A few kilometers beyond is the cliff-top, American-owned Hotel-Cabinas Playa Dominical, with clean, pleasant rooms at $10 per person. Public transportation in this area is poor.

Down toward Panama

The southern Pacific slope of Costa Rica was, until recently, isolated from the rest of the country. Before the 1950s, no highway crossed the Talamanca mountain range from the Central Valley, and all communication with the region was by a roundabout coastal land route that was mostly untraveled. What population there was concentrated in the banana regions around Golfito, which were tied by narrow-gauge railroad with Panama, and by steamship with the banana-consuming world.

With improved highway links, the inland valley of the General River has become one of the fastest-growing areas of Costa Rica. Many small farmers have migrated to this frontier region from the overcrowded lands of the Central Valley, with the encouragement and assistance of the government. The warm climate suits the valley to sugarcane and corn production, as well as cattle grazing.

The Pan American Highway runs south from San José up into

the Talamanca range and along the continental divide. The highest point on the whole Pan American Highway, 3355 meters above sea level, is near Cerro Buena Vista (Good-View Peak), known less optimistically as Cerro de la Muerte (Peak of Death). Both names are apt. When clouds are not clinging to the heights, the ride along the ridge, through a windblown landscape of stunted bushes and struggling tufts of grass, affords views to both the Pacific Ocean and the Caribbean. The second, more common name derives from the frigid climate, said to have killed many an oxcart driver.

SAN ISIDRO DE EL GENERAL

Population: Approximately 32,000; Altitude: 760 meters; 136 kilometers from San José.

San Isidro is the major town of the south, a transportation and farming center at the head of the General Valley. Though San Isidro was founded only in 1897, the area always had a scattered Indian population. The ride to San Isidro is more interesting than the town itself. One would come this way to continue overland to Panama, or to visit the national parks in the Talamanca range.

Buses for San Isidro depart from Calle 16, Avenidas 1/3 (Hotel Musoc), San José, every three hours from 4:30 a.m. to 4:30 p.m. The schedule in reverse is the same. Microbuses leave from across the street from the Hotel Musoc every three hours from 5:30 a.m. to 5:30 p.m. Again, the return schedule is the same. The trip takes about three hours.

The best accommodations in the area are at the 60-room Hotel del Sur (tel. 710233), outside of the city on the highway south, at Palmares. The rate is about $10 per person, and there is a pool. Cheaper and simpler accommodations are available at the Hotel Astoria (tel. 710914), Hotel Balboa (tel. 710606) and the Hotel Chirripó (tel. 710529).

Northeast of San Isidro, in the Talamanca mountains, are Chirripó National Park and La Amistad International Park, which stretches onward into Panama. Chirripó park includes Cerro Chirripó, at 3820 meters (12,530 feet) the highest mountain peak in the country. The habitat of the park ranges from rocky,

154

frigid heights and glacial lakes to the stunted, windblown vegetation of the harsh altitudes, known as paramo, to oak and evergreen forest, highland meadows and cloud forest. There are several trails to Chirripó peak, and shelters along the way. Horses are available to assist hikers with their gear. The ascent generally takes two days, with an early start the second morning to beat the clouds to the top. Climbers are rewarded with views not only of two oceans, but of the chain of mountain and volcanic peaks marching to the northwest toward San José. The park is 15 kilometers from San Isidro. Access is via bus or four-wheel-drive vehicle through the village of San Gerardo to the park entrance. Visits must be arranged through the park service headquarters in San José.

With the establishment of the huge La Amistad International Park, adjacent to Chirripó, Costa Rica doubled its national park lands. Most of La Amistad remains unexplored, and there are no services for visitors. Access is via a poor road through San Vito, near the Panamanian border.

After traversing the General Valley, the Pan American Highway follows the valley of the Río Grande de Terraba, down into sweltering banana lands. Around the town of Boruca is an area populated by indigenous peoples whose ancestors were relocated, under Spanish orders, from the slopes of the Talamanca range. A mission was set up here in 1626. One of the most notable Boruca activities was their practice of birth control, through means unknown to outsiders. The traditional fiesta of the Borucas is celebrated on February 8.

Farther along the road is Palmar Sur (232 kilometers from San José), known for *las bolas grandes,* the nearly perfectly spherical stone balls, ranging up to 2.5 meters in diameter, found on banana lands in the nearby Diquis Valley. Among the mysteries of the bolas: they are made of granite, but there is no naturally occurring granite nearby; it is harder to carve larger spheres accurately, yet the larger ones are more perfect than the smaller ones; few stone balls are nearly equal in size, which indicates that a template was probably not used in their manufacture; no datable artifacts have been discovered with the stone balls, which makes analysis and interpretation difficult. One suggestion is that the balls were used as burial-ground markers, but there is little creditable evidence to support this idea. Stone balls may be seen in the plaza of Palmar Sur, as well as at the national museum and in Carrillo Park in San José.

The Osa Peninsula, south of the Diquis Valley, is a wild area virtually devoid of roads. Only light planes, and boats running between Puerto Jiménez and Golfito, provide communication with the outside world.

Osa is a fabled area where, since the 1930s, a rough-and-ready breed of solitary prospectors has panned the streams and tunneled the hills for gold. These men from many countries have stayed in the wild for months, crossing paths with monkeys, snakes and mountain lions, and, more recently, teams of workers for large mining companies, equipped with heavy machinery.

Corcovado National Park, in the southern part of Osa, includes vast stretches of the only virgin rain forest in Central America. Among the natural treasures of Corcovado are trees of 500 species (including one kapok, or silk-cotton tree, that is the largest tree in Costa Rica); numerous endangered mammals, among them cougars, jaguars, ocelots, margays, yaguarundis and brocket deer; assorted monkeys and snakes; and peccaries, which may be the most destructive and dangerous species in the park. Vegetation zones range from mountain rain forest down to beach and fresh-water and mangrove swamps.

With its remote location, Corcovado attracts mainly scientific researchers. There are, however, extensive trails along the beach and in the forested interior, and camping is permitted. Abundant, easily viewed wildlife is the main attraction. Access to Corcovado is by light plane to park headquarters, or by hiking in, after crossing by boat from the mainland. Visits must be arranged through the National Park Service in San José.

Outside of the park, accommodations are available at Las Ventanas de Osa, a remote rain-forest lodge at the northwest edge of the Peninsula, named for the "windows" formed by waves beating against seaside cliffs. Facilities at this remote location are limited, but include a swimming pool, and 14 rooms in several buildings. The lodge sponsors three-day to week-long stays for approximately $190 per person per day, including all meals, jungle tours, and flight from San José to Palmar Sur. For information, write or call Las Ventanas de Osa, Box 820, Yellow-knife, N.W.T., Canada, X1A 2H2 (tel. 403-920-4100) or Natural History Tours, Box 2045, Kissimmee, Florida 32742 (tel. 904-228-3356).

Caño Island, 20 kilometers off the Osa Peninsula, was once used as a burial ground by coastal tribes. Numerous artifacts have been found, most notably small stone spheres. The variety of materials used in other objects suggests that long-distance maritime trade flourished before the Spaniards arrived. Caño Island, with its high forest, is now a biological reserve.

Coco Island, cliff-bordered and of volcanic origin, lies 500 kilometers southwest of the Costa Rican mainland. Abundant rainfall made Coco a watering place for ships in the colonial period. During the independence upheavals in Spanish America, the aristocracy of Peru entrusted its treasures to Captain James Thompson, who absconded and reputedly buried his loot on Coco Island. Treasure-seekers have periodically sought the cache, but all deny success (at least publicly). Coco Island is now a national park and is the home of three species of bird—the Coco Island finch, the Coco Island cuckoo, and Ridgeway's papamoscas —found nowhere else.

Golfito, on the Golfo Dulce (Sweet Gulf), is the last major town in the south, a banana port surrounded by lands that receive abundant rainfall all year. Flights to Golfito (departing from San José every day except Sunday at 6:50 a.m., returning at 8:20 a.m.) provide a relatively inexpensive shortcut on the route to Panama.

From Ciudad Neily, 17 kilometers from the border, a branch road leads up into the mountains to San Vito de Java, settled by Italian immigrants. Coffee is grown in the region.

Paso Canoas, 347 kilometers from San José, is the town on the border with Panama. Stores do a flourishing business with cross-border shoppers, but accommodations in the area are over-priced. Travelers should plan to get to the border early in the day in order to be able to move on.

Travel Information

GETTING TO COSTA RICA

By Air

From the United States, San José is served directly by LACSA, the Costa Rican airline (from Miami, New York and Los Angeles), Eastern Air Lines, and Challenge International (both from Miami). LACSA offers an interesting stopover in Guatemala on its routing from New York. Mexicana and SAHSA also provide service through intermediate points.

One-way tickets from Miami cost about $240. The fare drops to $300 round-trip, or even lower, for a stay of up to three weeks if you include a $50 ground package. The package need only consist of lodging at budget hotels for part of your stay. Fare structures are similar from other cities.

For current fare information and schedules call the airlines: Eastern (800-327-8376), Challenge (800-343-1222), LACSA (800-225-2272), Mexicana (800-531-7921) and SAHSA (800-327-1225). A creative travel agent can often obtain lower fares than those quoted directly by the airlines (see More Information for recommendations).

San José is also served daily by various airlines from all the Central American capitals, and weekly by KLM from Europe. The SAM airlines flight from San José to the Colombian island of San Andrés is one of the cheaper ways to continue to South America.

Remember that you may have to show an onward or return ticket to satisfy the immigration authorities in San José.

Tickets purchased in Costa Rica are subject to a 10 percent sales tax, and in most cases must be paid for in dollars.

Driving

The shortest highway distance from Brownsville, Texas, to San José, Costa Rica, is about 2250 miles. For the vast majority of travelers, who have limited vacation time, it's simply not worthwhile to consider driving, with six borders to cross, difficult mountain roads, and fears of political turmoil and breakdowns en route.

However. . . if you're going south for the winter, if you're planning to spend time elsewhere in Central America as well, if you're camping, if you happen to be continuing onward to South America, or if your vehicle is simply indispensable, driving may be indicated. Rest assured that getting to Costa Rica is eminently possible.

Your major requirement is a vehicle in good shape. Have it checked out, tuned up and greased before you leave home. Replace cracked or withering belts and hoses, bald tires and rusting brake lines. If you're planning extensive travel off the main roads, consider taking a couple of spare tires, a gasoline can, water for you and the radiator, points, plugs, electrical tape, belts, wire, and basic tools. Otherwise, there's no reason to prepare for a safari, and the family sedan will serve you well. Be prepared to disconnect your catalytic converter south of Mexico, where unleaded gasoline is not available.

Avoid extra fees by crossing borders during regular business hours, generally from 8 a.m. to noon and from 2 p.m. to 6 p.m. It's prudent to travel during daylight hours only, to avoid stray animals and inebriated humans. Fill your tank whenever you can—gas stations can be few and far between. Plan your route to avoid transiting El Salvador—a direct crossing from Guatemala to Honduras is possible.

Essential documents for entry to any Central American country are your regular driver's license, vehicle registration, and passport with visa. Mexican insurance is available at all entry points. Vehicle insurance available in Guatemala is generally valid for all of Central America, but make sure this applies to the policy you buy. Vehicle permits for Costa Rica are issued at the border, are valid for 30 days, and *may not be renewed.* Drivers wishing to stay longer must take their vehicles out of the country for two days.

Maps of Mexico and Central America are available from your

local automobile club. Maps of Costa Rica and Central America are available from the Costa Rican Tourist Board (see "More Information," below).

Bus

The disadvantages of bus travel all the way to Costa Rica are obvious—long hours in a sitting position, inconvenient connections, border delays, and much else. You can, however, see much along the way, and the price is right. Total fare from the U. S. border to Costa Rica is less than $75, and this may be reduced by using less comfortable, slower, second-class local buses. Overland travel will require that you pick up visas in advance for all the countries you'll be transiting.

Some specifics: First class buses, similar to Greyhound units, operate from all U. S. border points to Mexico City, a trip of from 10 hours to two days, depending on your crossing point. Buses of the Cristóbal Colón line depart Mexico City at least twice daily for the Guatemalan border, sixteen hours away, connecting with buses for Guatemala City. From there, the Tica Bus line provides through service to Costa Rica. The trip through Mexico may be shortened by following the Gulf coast route via Veracruz from eastern Texas, avoiding Mexico City.

ENTERING COSTA RICA

Citizens of the United States must have a tourist card or a passport and visa to enter Costa Rica.

Tourist cards are issued by airlines serving Costa Rica and by Costa Rican consulates upon presentation of a birth certificate, passport, or other substantial identification. Tourist cards cost $2 and are valid for 30 days. Monthly extensions to up to six months from the date of entry may be obtained at the immigration department in San José.

Visas are issued at no charge by Costa Rican consulates. Visa holders also must apply for permission to stay in Costa Rica for more than 30 days. Visas are required for overland travel to Costa Rica.

Canadians may enter Costa Rica with a passport only. Entry will usually be authorized for 90 days, with monthly extensions available for another 90 days.

Travelers from the following countries may also enter Costa Rica with a passport and no visa: Austria, Belgium, Colombia, Denmark, Luxembourg, El Salvador, Guatemala, Holland, Honduras, Italy, Nicaragua, Norway, Panama, Portugal, Liechtenstein, the United Kingdom, West Germany, Sweden, Switzerland, Yugoslavia, Argentina, Japan, Spain, Finland, France, Brazil and Rumania.

Travelers from other countries, and all business travelers, must have a passport and visa.

All tourists may be required to show $150 upon arrival, as well as a return or onward ticket.

Tourist cards and permits to stay in Costa Rica (for those traveling on a passport) may be extended by application to the immigration department (Migración), Calle 21, Avenidas 6/8. Processing an extension can take a few days. Some travel agents will take care of the paperwork, for a fee.

Note that Costa Rican immigration officials no longer exclude travelers with back packs. They are still sensitive to appearance, however, both at entry points and at headquarters in San José. A sprucing-up will help your case.

Land borders are officially open from 6:30 a.m. to 11 a.m., 12:30 p.m. to 5:30 p.m. and 6:30 p.m. to 10 p.m.

Customs

Visitors are allowed to enter Costa Rica with any used personal possessions that they will reasonably need, including sports equipment. The exemption for new merchandise is $100 of customs duty. New merchandise may include up to three liters of liquor, one pound of tobacco, and six rolls of film.

Returning Home

U. S. Customs allows an exemption of $400 per person in goods, including one quart of liquor and 200 cigarettes. Canadian residents may use their once-yearly $300 exemption, or their $100 quarterly exemption for goods brought home, with a limit of 1.1 liters of liquor and 200 cigarettes.

Costa Rica prohibits the export of pre-Columbian artifacts. In practice, there is a flourishing black market in these items, and there is limited official concern for pieces of little artistic value. Once should be careful, however, not least because many artifacts are phony.

GETTING AROUND

By Air

Costa Rica's domestic airline, SANSA, operates flights to a number of outlying towns from Juan Santamaría International Airport. Latest flight frequencies are as follows:

To Guápiles, Limón, Quepos and Golfito, six times weekly; to Tamarindo and Liberia, three times weekly. Flights are also available at times to Barra del Colorado, via Limón.

Fares are reasonable by most standards: $20 to Tamarindo, $29 to Barra del Colorado, for example.

Recent schedules are given in coverage of towns in this book. For latest schedules and fares, contact the SANSA office at Calle 24, Avenidas Central /1, tel 333258.

Charter flights in small planes are also available from Tobías Bolaños airport (just west of San José) to places without regularly scheduled service, such as Tortuguero National Park. Arrange such flights through travel agencies, or directly through the companies listed in the yellow pages under "Aviación."

By Bus

There are several tiers of bus service in Costa Rica. Depending on where you are in the country and how far you're going, getting around by bus can be pleasant and comfortable, tolerable, or—if you're not prepared—an ordeal.

Service between towns in the Central Valley is provided by large buses similar to those used on the city lines in San José. These generally have padded seats, which are closer together than those in comparable American buses, but comfortable enough for the distances involved.

Fares on suburban routes are generally fixed, no matter how far you travel. On routes covering a few towns, you'll pay according to how far you go. Fare cards are often posted near the driver's seat.

Buses in the Central Valley may be boarded either at their terminals, or at bus stops, which are marked either by shelters

162

or short yellow lines painted along the edge of the road. Pay the driver, choose a seat, and enjoy the sights along the way.

Buses operating on the major highways between San José and the far points of the country are roughly comparable to Greyhound buses in the United States. They may be older, and lack air conditioning and lavatories, but they are generally well cared for and kept mechanically sound.

Drivers of long-distance buses try to maintain the maximum possible speed, even on winding roads. Bus crews are ready for such side affects as nausea with plastic bags (comforting). Prepare yourself with motion sickness pills if you're susceptible.

Tickets for long-distance buses may be purchased in advance, and this is recommended for weekend travel. If you try to board a long-distance bus along its route, it may or may not stop— there's no fixed rule. Try to select a waiting place where the driver will see you well in advance and have a chance to slow down. Ask a handy local for advice.

Buses operating in rural areas outside the Central Valley are of an entirely different breed. Most are similar to American school buses. Some in fact *are* old school buses, right down to the yellow paint. (Old school buses never die. They just go to Central America.) Seats are stiff, with minimal padding, designed for small people traveling short distances.

Rural buses stop frequently to let out and pick up passengers, as well as chickens, cardboard boxes full of merchandise, and whatever else has to move. Add poor roads and steep grades, and a trip of fifty kilometers may take a couple of hours. Many a passenger has to stand in a crowded aisle, for there is often no other way to go.

Country people in Costa Rica are used to conditions on buses, and may even doze off, despite the bouncing and shaking and cramped quarters. Without precautions, however, the visitor may find rural bus trips excruciating. Some tips for enjoying, or at least surviving, your trip:

Look for a place where you can stretch your legs. The seat behind the driver is usually best. If it's not available, try an aisle seat, even if this costs you some views. Get to the bus terminal early to be sure of getting a seat at all.

Sit toward the front of the bus—the shaking is always worse at the rear.

By all means, go to the bathroom before you get on the bus (nobody else will tell you this), and don't drink too much coffee or any other liquid before you set out.

Rural buses will generally stop anyplace you flag them down. Pay the driver or his helper, and call out "parada!" to get the bus to stop.

Fares on all buses in Costa Rica are low, generally less than two cents (U. S.) per kilometer.

Automobile

Driving is a fine way to get around parts of Costa Rica, especially the Central Valley, where expressways connect the major towns. Distances to be covered are short, and you can take it easy and enjoy the scenery. But driving can be expensive. Gasoline prices and car rental rates are more than twice those in the United States.

In the Central Valley, roads are well marked with standard rectangular signs. In the center of any town, signs point the way toward the next towns in all directions, and usually indicate distances. Hazard signs use easily understood symbols.

Main routes outside the Central Valley are also well marked, but secondary roads are not. Navigation is made even more difficult by the lack of accurate, up-to-date road maps. Ask directions at junctions if you have any doubts. Gasoline stations (bombas) are sparse, so fill up before turning off any main route. While you're at it, inquire about road conditions ahead.

Costa Rica's mountain roads are probably more winding than any you're used to. Beep you horn at curves and drive at moderate speeds. The driver going up a hill has the right of way, so be prepared to pull over or back up on narrow stretches.

Many auto parts are hard to obtain outside of San José. Try to have your car serviced and repairs made in the capital or nearby. Parts for some makes of car are simply not stocked in Costa Rica, but drivers of most Japanese and smaller American cars should have no problems in this regard.

Taxis

It doesn't occur to most people, but taxis are a very practical way to get around the countryside in Costa Rica. Current official rates are 70 cents for the first kilometer, 25 cents for each additional kilometer, and $3.00 per hour of waiting time. A 120-kilometer round trip from San José to Poás volcano should run less than $30, including a couple of hours of waiting, which compares favorably to the cost of renting a car. In addition, you'll be able to look around instead of keeping your eyes glued to the road, and can direct the driver to slow down or stop where you please.

Travel by taxi is not without its problems. Many drivers are used to overcharging tourists, which is easy to do, since few taxis have meters. Look for a driver who will agree to charge the official rates (which your hotel can confirm), or at least not too much more.

For long-distance travel, of course, you'll want to use airplanes or comfortable buses. But taxis are a good bet for going those last few kilometers in rural areas. In the Nicoya Peninsula and other areas with poor roads, taxis are usually jeeps or similar vehicles well suited to local conditions.

Tours and Packages

Descriptions of the tours that you may book when in Costa Rica are given in the coverage of San José in this book.

Packages of hotel, meal and tour arrangements that you arrange when you buy your airplane ticket vary from three-night plans that cover only your hotel and a city tour of San José, for $50 per person, to complete arrangements for a week or more of hotels, meals, excursions to the coasts, volcano trips, and/or fishing. The principal advantage of the low-price packages is that they allow you to take advantages of cheaper airfares. The more complete packages, of course, spare you much planning and attention to details. Rarely do they save you money.

Packages are best booked through a travel agent. If yours is not familiar with Costa Rica, request information from the Costa Rica Tourist Board (see "More Information," below). For special-interest programs, such as hiking, write directly to the agencies listed in the San José section. Tours with an emphasis on wildlife are offered by Journeys, Box 2658, Ann Arbor, MI 48106, tel. 800-255-8735, 313-655-4407.

ASSORTED PRACTICAL INFORMATION

Business Hours

Businesses generally open at 9 a.m., close for a couple of hours starting at 11:30 a.m. or noon, then open for the afternoon from 1:30 or 2 p.m. until 6 p.m. On Saturdays, many businesses are open in the morning only. In the hotter lowlands along the Atlantic and Pacific, stores open earlier, and the midday break is longer. You'll soon get used to doing your shopping before or after the break, or rest *(descanso),* which, by the way, is rarely called a siesta.

During December, as Christmas bonuses are spent, normal hours are abandoned, and many stores remain open throughout the day, and even on Sunday morning.

Bureaucracy

(This comes first alphabetically, but I don't want to start this section on an unpleasant note.)

All countries have their problems—natural disasters, human rights violations, racial tensions, refugees, whatever. Costa Rica has its bureaucracy. When you put it in perspective, it seems a minor matter. To deal with it, however, is deadly.

Costa Ricans are use to runarounds and frustrations in government and commerce. Processing insurance claims, obtaining nonemergency health care, and receiving payments for officially marketed crops all can involve inexplicable delays. Seekers of licenses must peck patiently at the roosts of officialdom. Queues as orderly as any in London form at bus stops, government offices, and even at the entrances to supermarkets. Standing in line is an honorable profession and source of employment in Costa Rica. Many businesses have one or more *mensajeros* (messengers) for this purpose. Their badge of office is a motorcycle helmet.

Visitors may think that they are exempt from engagement with the domestic bureaucratic mentality, and in most cases they are. Some exposure, however, is inevitable. See "Money and Banking," below, for an example.

Calendars

Some Costa Rican holidays, such as Christmas and Easter, will be known to most visitors. But you can't be expected to be aware of a favorite saint's special day. Take a quick look at the list of public holidays below. If any occur while you're in Costa Rica, don't plan to get anything done on that day except relaxing.

January 1	New Year's Day
March 19	Day of St. Joseph (San José)
Moveable	Holy Thursday
Moveable	Good Friday (Many businesses close all of Holy Week)
April 11	Battle of Rivas
May 1	Labor Day
Moveable	Corpus Christi
June 29	Day of Sts. Peter and Paul
July 25	Annexation of Guanacaste
August 2	Day of Our Lady of the Angels (specially celebrated in Cartago)
August 15	Assumption Day
September 15	Independence Day
October 12	Columbus Day (Día de la Raza)
December 8	Immaculate Conception
December 24 and 25	Christmas Eve and Christmas
December 31	New Year's Eve

In addition to the above, all towns celebrate the feast day of their patron saint—San Marcos (St. Mark) on April 25, Santiago (St. James) on July 25, etc. Images of the patron saint are borne from the town church in processions, but most of the celebrants' efforts go into the parades of masked figures, raffles, bingo, dances, banquets, drinking and benign bullfights that make these occasions breaks from the humdrum round of chores. And the Christmas-New Year season is a time of extended street celebration everywhere, especially in San José.

Children

Costa Rica is one of the more benign countries to which you can take children. Health and sanitary standards are acceptable, there are sights and activities for kids as well as grownups, and few people give you funny looks if you take children to restaurants, museums, or anywhere else.

Special health concerns for children are few. If you're going to spend time at the beach, make sure that your child gets plenty to drink, and limit exposure to the sun. In general, follow the same precautions for children as for adults (see a few pages ahead).

Pack clothing items similar to those for adults. As well, take a few books and toys (the latter are expensive locally), including a pail and shovel for the beach. Take baby wipes for quick cleanups. Children need their own identification for immigration purposes.

For babies, take changing supplies and bottle-feeding equipment, if needed. Disposable diapers are available in Costa Rica, but cost double what they do in the States, so you may want to pack these, too. A stroller is useful in the cities, a cloth carrier at the beach. Cribs are available in most of the better hotels and you should be able to improvise in the few cases where you won't find them.

Gerber baby foods (instant cereals and strained vegetables and meat) are manufactured in Costa Rica, and are sold in pharmacies and supermarkets in San José and the larger towns. Other readily available food items for babies include canned condensed milk, canned fruit juice, cheeses, fruits, and powdered formulas.

With kids in tow, you'll spend considerable time in your hotel room. Be more selective than you might otherwise be. A television in the room and a swimming pool are attractive amenities for the kids, even if you don't need them for yourself.

Hotels in Costa Rica rarely charge for children up to three years old. Older children will pay a small extra-bed charge, or half the adult rate if meals are included.

Climate

Despite tropical latitudes, climate in Costa Rica varies from near-frigid to humid and sweltering, according to the influence of mountain barriers, altitude and prevailing winds.

The highland climate of the major cities—San José, Cartago, Heredia and Alajuela—is often called "eternal spring," a term that is not used merely to attract tourists. Temperatures are in the low 70s Fahrenheit (about 22 degrees Centigrade) during the day throughout the year. The high mountains and volcanoes to the north of San José block the clouds that blow in from the Atlantic, and it rains only from April to November or December, when winds are from the Pacific. But a long rainy day is a rarity in the Central Valley. Mornings are generally clear, followed by a few hours of heavy downpour in the afternoon. Sometimes the rain can last into the night. Clouds hold in the heat of the day, and nights are generally warm. The rainy season is called *invierno* (winter), even though Costa Rica is in the northern hemisphere. In the dry times, or *verano* (summer), days are uniformly warm and sunny. Nights are clear, and the temperature may sometimes drop into the fifties (about 10 degrees Centigrade).

Down toward the Pacific coast, the climate is hotter. In Puntarenas, daytime temperatures are in the nineties (above 32 degrees Centigrade) throughout the year. But at the beaches, refreshing breezes moderate the heat. The rainy season is the same as in the Central Valley, but precipitation is heavier. The exceptions are the extreme north and extreme south. The Guanacaste plain suffers periodic droughts, which bother farmers more than visitors. And around Golfito, near Panama, peculiarities in the mountains and winds bring rains throughout the year.

On the Atlantic slope of Costa Rica, storms may blow in at any time, though rainfall is lightest from February through April. Precipitation is over ten feet at Limón in most years, and even higher to the north. Storms appear suddenly and with a frightening fury, but they are usually quickly gone. Temperatures are generally as hot on the Caribbean as on the Pacific, and the humidity is more enervating.

The higher altitudes are cooler. Frosts occur above 2150 meters (7000 feet) during the dry season. And atop volcanoes and in the Talamanca mountains, temperatures may plunge from warm to below freezing in a few hours.

Keep the climate in mind when you pack for your visit. Take

169

a raincoat or umbrella if you'll be outdoors a lot during the rainy season, or if you're heading toward the Caribbean. Taking shelter from the rain for a few hours, however, is no special inconvenience, and during the dry season, around San José and along most of the Pacific, not even the thought of rain occurs.

Cost of Living

It will be obvious from prices mentioned in this book that travel expenses in Costa Rica are moderate. Middle-range hotel rooms cost $40 to $50 double in San José, but clean, airy rooms are available for as little as $20 for two. Outside San José, except at deluxe beach hotels, room rates are generally lower.

Two dollars will buy a basic, wholesome meal in San José, while a gourmet-quality repast may carry a tab of $10 or more, not including wine, which is expensive. Outside the Central Valley, fine cuisine is usually not available, and basic meals may cost somewhat more.

While automobile ownership and maintenance are expensive (except for retired foreigners, who may import a car duty-free), public transport is not. The bus fare from San José to any border point is less than $5. Scheduled flights in small planes cost less than $30 to the most distant towns. Hiring a taxi costs about the same as renting a car, or less.

Foreigners who live in Costa Rica find that they save considerable amounts on services and housing, and on the heavy clothing and other items that they can live without because of the mild climate.

Heat and air conditioning are unnecessary in most well-built houses in San José. Many a comfortable home has a fireplace more for esthetic than practical reasons. Lower land taxes and insurance rates further reduce fixed costs. Electric rates are not the bargain they once were—they now compare with those in the eastern United States—but with fewer appliances, consumption is generally much lower. Household workers are generally paid $100 per month, or less.

Houses cost roughly half what they do in the United States, sometimes less. But comparisons in this respect are imperfect. The housing market has lately been depressed in Costa Rica, and construction methods are different. Most houses come without the appliances and built-in closets and cabinets that one

170

expects in the States, and electrical wiring and plumbing standards are lower. Rental housing is reasonably priced. Two-bedroom apartments with some furnishings go for as little as $250 per month, though in exclusive areas the tab may be much, much higher.

The crunch, when it comes, is in consumer goods. Tape recorders, home computers, cameras, watches, appliances, and almost every other imported, manufactured item costs double to triple what it does in the States. Clothing of local manufacture is priced slightly higher than similar American items. Cosmetics, whether locally made or imported, are pricey.

At the supermarkets, many packaged and processed items cost more than in the States, while fresh foods cost the same or less. By adjusting eating patterns, one can usually end up with a lower food bill.

Here is a rather unscientific sampling of prices for grocery and non-grocery items at a San José supermarket:

Meat, one-third less than U. S. prices; fish, one-half to same; cosmetics and diapers, double or higher; local canned foods, same to one-half more; imported canned foods, double or more; eggs, one-half higher; coffee, two-thirds less; dairy products, slightly less; beer, same; fruit and vegetables in season, same to two-thirds less; Gerber baby foods, same to one-third more. Some specific recent prices: cigarettes, 50 cents per pack; local brands of liquor, $3 per 750 ml bottle; fruit wine (not very good), $1.50; imported wines, $6 and up for drinkable stuff; Scotch whiskey, $9 and up; Spanish brandy, $20.

In general, persons who are not too attached to mechanical gadgets and pre-packaged, processed foods can maintain a comfortable standard of living for less than in the United States.

Electricity is supplied at 110 volts, alternating current, throughout Costa Rica. Sockets are of the American type, usually without provision for a grounding prong. Non-grounded American and Canadian appliances should work without adapters. However, it's always wise to ask about the voltage in your hotel before you plug anything in. In remote locations, generators may operate on a non-standard voltage.

Fishing

The marvels of sport fishing in the mountain streams and off both coasts of Costa Rica are still a recent discovery, at least for non-Costa Ricans. Stocks of fish are plentiful, and records are regularly approached, and broken.

On the Caribbean side of Costa Rica, the most notorious species is the pesky and finicky tarpon. Tarpon are caught between January and June in rivers, lagoons and estuaries, and weigh as much as 100 pounds. Other species common to the Caribbean are snook, usually weighing over 25 pounds; the smaller, bass-like machaca and guapote; mojarra, which resembles a bluegill; and shark, mackerel, mullet and jack crevalle. All are found in inland waters, even shark. Deep sea fishing in the Caribbean is limited by the unpredictability of storms.

On the Pacific side, black and blue marlins of up to 1000 pounds are the big attractions, along with sailfish, roosterfish, dolphin, wahoo, rainbow runner, barracuda, a variety of snappers and jacks, pompano, shark, swordfish, yellowfin tuna, bonito, grouper and corvina, or sea bass. The smaller fish are found in river mouths and estuaries, the larger species out in blue water.

Inland, some of Costa Rica's mountain streams hold trout and smaller fish.

Fishing equipment is in short supply, so serious anglers should bring their own gear, whether they will be fishing from a camp or from one of the Pacific coast hotels. Fishing camps (mentioned in the coverage of the Caribbean and Pacific coastal areas) will recommend specific types of rods, reels and line to take along.

A permit is required for fishing. If you book a week at a fishing camp, the management will probably take care of this detail. Otherwise, you'll have to buy a permit for $10 at the Central Bank (Calle 2, Avenidas 1/Central, San José). For offshore fishing, present it for validation with two passport photos to the fishing office (Oficina de Pesca) of the Ministry of Agriculture, Old La Salle Building, La Sabana, San José, office number 33. For river fishing, the permit is validated at the Wildlife Office (Oficina de Vida Silvestre) at Avenida 2 and Calle 6, San José (above the Kentucky Fried Chicken restaurant).

Flora and Fauna

Costa Rican flora and fauna, and tropical flora and fauna in general, are too varied to be treated justly in a small section of this book, or even in a few books devoted exclusively to the subject. Botanists refer to the natural exuberance of the tropics as "species richness." An area that supports two or three types of trees in the temperate zones may lodge dozens or even hundreds of plant species from ground level to forest canopy in the tropics. Some dimensions of this natural abundance in Costa Rica: More than 2000 species of trees have so far been catalogued, twice as many as in the continental United States. Two-thirds of all known seed plants are found in Costa Rica. And there are over 1000 orchids, ranging from the guaria morada, the purple national flower, down to those with blossoms too tiny to be casually noticed; more than 800 species of fern; and so on, and so on.

One explanation of this variety takes into account the poverty of many tropical soils, which may encourage plants to adapt to compete for nourishment at all levels, up to the tops of the tallest trees. Some draw nutrients from the soil, others feed themselves by sending roots into neighboring plants as parasites, or by capturing dust and decay washed down by rain. All nutrients are continually recycled. Abundant water helps to make this many-tiered world possible. Plants take moisture from the earth, the rain, from pools in large leaves, and from the very humidity of the air around them.

This general tropical description applies to much of the Caribbean lowlands of Costa Rica, and to cloud forest at high elevations. The temperate central valley, with its grassy meadows, pine forests, and rich volcanic soil, will not appear exotic to most visitors. But even here, a number of trees flourish that are so unfamiliar as to be without names in English. The Pacific lowlands, also with rich soil, support their own varieties of forest, which vary according to rainfall.

Here is a rather random sample of wild and cultivated trees and plants found at different altitudes:

Sea level to 2000 feet: Palms (coconut, African oil, American oil, etc.), mangrove, mahogany, cedar, laurel, quinine, banana, rubber, walnut, guanacaste earpod, silk cotton (ceiba), cotton, cacao, sugarcane, rice, bamboo.

2000 to 6000 feet: coffee, corn, beans, pasture grass, wild fig (amate), orchids and bromeliads, citrus, avocado, mango, cactus, pomegranate, papaya.

6000 feet and higher: pine, fir (silvertree, spruce, etc.), cypress, alder, madrone, potato, peach, apple.

Many of the plant species of Costa Rica are described in *The National Parks of Costa Rica* (Madrid: INCAFO, 1981), available in San José. Additional species are mentioned in the coverage of national parks in this book.

As a bridge between two continents, Costa Rica is home to animal forms both familiar and exotic. More than 750 species of bird inhabit Costa Rica, as many as in all of the United States. These range from common jays and orioles to large-beaked toucans and macaws, and the exquisite and elusive long-tailed quetzals of the trogon family. The national list includes 50 species of hummingbird, 45 tanagers and 72 flycatchers.

Monkeys abound, among them howler, spider, white-faced and the tiny marmoset. White-tailed deer, raccoons and rattle-snakes, all common in North America, live alongside their South American cousins, the brocket deer, coatimundi and bushmaster. Sea turtles, alligators, peccaries, tepezcuintles (pacas, or spotted cavies), jaguars, ocelots, pumas and many other "exotic" species are common in parts of the country.

Paradoxically, many of these species are difficult to sight. In settled areas, native species of animal as well as plant have been wiped out by hunting, land-clearing and poaching. In less-settled areas, the lack of roads and trails keeps out the interested visitor. Fortunately, however, many species may be seen in Costa Rica's national parks (see below).

Food

Costa Rica's food holds few surprises. Most restaurants in San José serve what they call "international cuisine," which is a combination of standard North American and European food. *Bistec* (beef), *pollo* (chicken) and *pescado* (fish) are most often encountered on the menu, usually in forms that need little explanation. Genuine native-style food is enjoyed at home, in a very rare city restaurant that advertises its *comida típica* (native food), in simple country eateries, and as snacks.

One of the most common plates in the countryside is *casado*, fish, meat or chicken married ("casado") to rice, beans, and chopped cabbage. *Gallo pinto,* rice and beans, is the staple of poor people's diets, usually served with *tortillas,* flat cakes made of ground, lime-soaked corn. But you don't have to be poor to enjoy the taste of black beans and tortillas, or of *olla de carne* (a stew of beef, yucca and plantain), *chiles rellenos* (stuffed peppers), *chilasquiles* (meat-filled tortillas) or *pozol* (corn soup). You merely have to search these dishes out, if you're not part of a Costa Rican household. The Cosina de Leña is one San José restaurant that challenges the prejudice against eating Costa Rica's soul food in public.

Traditional snack foods are easier to find. Vendors sell *pan de yuca* (yucca bread), *gallos* (tortillas with fillings), *arreglados* (bread filled with meat and vegetables), *empanadas* (pastry stuffed with meat or some other filling), and various other starchy items at markets, on trains and at bus terminals. Other favorite snacks are tropical fruits (papayas, bananas, passionfruit, pineapple and many others) sold from carts everywhere in the country, and *pipas,* young juice coconuts. *Pejivalle,* a pasty palm fruit, and *palmito,* heart of palm, are enjoyed as hor d'oeuvres or in salad. Hot sauces and peppers—*chiles*— are condiments to be added as desired, and rarely included in a dish before serving.

Costa Rica's excellent coffee, of course, is enjoyed with all meals, and is often prepared by pouring hot water through grounds held in a sock-like device. Costa Ricans claim all kinds of special properties for their brew—it won't keep you up at night, nor jangle your nerves, but will stimulate you to overall better functioning. This is only understandable chauvinism. Sometimes coffee is served with sugar already added—specify without *(sin azúcar)* if your prefer it that way. *Café con leche* (coffee with milk) is at least half milk. The concept of coffee with cream is understood only in hotels and restaurants that have a foreign clientele.

Gourmet restaurants in San José and suburbs cook tender meats to order and serve them in delicate sauces along with crisp vegetables. Chinese, German, French, Italian, Swiss and even the better "international" restaurants produce superb results with foods that are fresh and abundant throughout the year. At the less expensive eateries in San José, and in the countryside, culi-

175

nary arts and sciences are, unfortunately, not widely diffused. What you'll find can most generously be described as home-style cooking—wholesome, reasonably priced, but not finely prepared —comparable to the fare at Joe's Diner. A *bistec* (steak) will generally be a tough, nondescript slab of meat, served with some of the grease in which it was cooked. The fate of fresh seafood is often similar. Vegetables, other than rice, beans and cabbage, when they are served, will have been in the pot for too long. None of this will do you any harm, especially when you pay only two to four dollars for your meal. At a few coastal resorts, standards are as high as in San José. But generally, when you leave the capital, you should lower your expectations.

Fortunately, almost every small town in Costa Rica has a Chinese restaurant, if not two or three, where *chao mein* (chow mein), chop suey and more elaborate plates tease bored palates. These restaurants are not gourmet-class, but they work interesting and edible combinations from Costa Rica's fresh vegetables and meats.

Service in Costa Rican restaurants is relaxed. You'll never be presented with a bill and ushered toward the cash register in order to make way for the next customer. The pleasures of lingering over nothing more than a pastry and a cup of coffee can still be enjoyed. If leisurely dining isn't what you have in mind, you'll have to call the waiter over in order to place your order, and to ask for the bill *(la cuenta)*. A ten-percent tax and a ten-percent service charge will be added on.

Costa Rican eating and drinking habits in restaurants may be disorienting. As you have your morning coffee and bacon and eggs, the Tico to the left of you will be starting the day with a whiskey and a chicken sandwich. The Tico to the right of you will be cutting into a steak, accompanied by a beer. The Tico in front of you enjoys a rum and Coke while he ponders the menu. You are too polite (or dumbfounded) to turn to the Tico behind you.

I have no explanations for these customs, except to state that restaurant food is not necessarily derived from what is traditionally eaten at home. *You* were taught that eggs are eaten at breakfast. Maybe they were not. Explaining an affection for liquor is a touchy thing, but there is no doubt that Costa Ricans enjoy their booze in large quantities and at varied hours.

Much of what is consumed is *guaro,* which can be roughly translated as "hootch." Guaro is the cheapest liquor, distilled from sugarcane, and sold in bars for 15 and 30 cents a shot. Sugarcane is also the base for rums of various qualities and agings, some of them quite good. Most guaros and rums are distilled by a government-owned factory, but other companies make quite drinkable vodkas and gins. Local whiskeys and liqueurs are also available, but their quality is not as high. The exception is Café Rica, a coffee liqueur, which costs more than other Costa Rican drinks. Imported alcoholic drinks are quite expensive (with the exception of whiskey, which is only moderately expensive at about $10 per fifth), so if you have a favorite brand, bring a bottle or two or three with you. Rum and Coke (Cuba Libre) is Costa Rica's most popular mixed drink.

Local fruit wines are interesting for amusement, but are not taken seriously by anyone who has enjoyed wine elsewhere. Imported wines are quite a luxury. Wine drinkers will have to fork out the money (a few duty-free bottles won't go very far), or else switch to another drink for the duration.

An excellent alternative to wine is beer. Pilsen is a superb brand of beer (in my opinion), and Tropical and Bavaria are almost as good. There are various others to suit different tastes. A beer in a restaurant rarely costs more than 75 cents.

Bars are generally the cheapest places to drink, and they serve a dividend: *bocas.* These are hor d'oeuvres that may range from cheese and crackers to little sandwiches that, over enough rounds, will constitute a meal in themselves.

The easiest place to buy liquor, beer or wine is at a super-market. In small towns with no supermarkets, try the bars them-selves or small general stores (pulperías), though the selection will be more limited. The deposit on a beer or soda bottle is usually as much as the price of what's inside.

Health Concerns

The health worries that usually accompany a trip to Latin America—mad dashes to the bathroom, general malaise as un-known microbes attack your insides, long-forgotten diseases like typhoid turning up in the best hotels—hardly apply to Costa Rica, where sanitary standards are generally high and most people are educated enough to have an idea of how disease spreads. Good sense and normal caution should be enough to see you through Costa Rica in good health.

No special inoculations or vaccinations are required or recommended for visitors to Costa Rica. You should, however, get your health affairs in order before you travel. Catch up on immunizations, such as those for tetanus and polio, and consult your doctor if any condition or suspected condition, such as an ear infection, might trouble you during air travel. Take along the medicines that you use regularly, and an extra pair of prescription glasses.

Water in San José and in most of the towns of the Central Valley is chemically treated and safe to drink. Elsewhere, inquire, and if you're still not sure or are simply cautious, stick to bottled sodas or beer. Suspect water is easily treated with laundry bleach (two drops per quart, let stand 30 minutes). Limit exposure to sun if you haven't seen any for a while, and take along some insect repellent for the west coast in the rainy season, and for the Caribbean at any time. Also, take it easy on alcohol until you become accustomed to the higher altitude in San José.

For extensive travel at the budget level or off the beaten track, a dose of immunoglobulin for protection against hepatitis and a typhoid booster are advisable. If you're heading to rural parts of the Caribbean lowlands, take a weekly dosage of a malaria preventative, such as Aralen. Budget travelers should avoid fleabag hotels. Fleas and similar insects are not only unpleasant in themselves but can carry disease. If both top and bottom sheets are not clean and clean-smelling, move on.

How to Get into Trouble

It's not too likely that you'll get into hot water while visiting Costa Rica. But some customs and practices may differ from what you're use to. Relax and act as if you're on vacation, while keeping in mind some possible sore points.

Drugs, of course, are a touchy item, especially when used by foreigners. Penalties for possession of anything from marijuana on up are severe, so abstention or at least discretion is advised.

Costa Rica is a democracy, but quite security-conscious, more than ever now that the countries to the north are in turmoil. Visitors may be asked for identification at any time, and jailed (yes!) if they do not have proper papers. Always carry your passport or tourist card with you, and arrange prompt replacement if either is lost or stolen.

Take normal precautions against petty theft. Carry your money in an inside pocket, when possible, and be especially careful on crowded streets and when leaving banks.

There are many stories of foreigners having been ripped off, sometimes for considerable amounts of money, in real estate purchases and investment schemes. Be more cautious than at home before parting with your money. You will probably have no legal recourse if your money evaporates in a flurry of documents and contracts that you don't understand.

Language Schools

The advantage of studying Spanish in a country where the language is spoken are obvious. A number of schools in Costa Rica offer Spanish-language instruction in small groups or on an individual basis. A four-week package of study, room and meals in a private home, and escorted trips around the country, costs about $900. Half-day instruction in small groups for a month, without accommodations, will run about $300. Write or call the language schools for brochures and current prices. A partial listing:

Centro Lingüístico Conversa, Apartado 17, San José, tel. 217649. Courses in San José and at a farm west of the city.

Instituto de Idiomas, Edificio Victoria, Avenida 3, Calles 3/5, San José, tel. 239662.

Instituto Interamericano de Idiomas Intensa, P. O. Box 8110, Calle 33, Avenidas 5/7 (no. 540), Barrio Escalante, San José, tel. 256009.

Centro Cultural Costarricense-Norteamericano, Calle 37, San Pedro (suburban San José), tel. 259485.

A number of U.S. and Canadian universities offer Spanish study programs in San José. Inquire for details at the Spanish department of a university near your home.

Money and Banking

Costa Rica's unit of currency is the colón, which is named

after Christopher Columbus (Colón in Spanish). Each colón is divided into 100 céntimos. In slang usage, the colón is sometimes called a peso.

In this book, I've quoted most prices in U. S. dollars, based on the current rate of exchange, which is about 65 colones to the dollar. Costa Rica's currency has an unstable recent history, and a different rate of exchange may be in effect at the time of your visit. You may even find that some prices, in U. S. dollar terms, are lower than those I've indicated. Most hotel rooms, however, are priced directly in U. S. dollars, so you can expect little variation in these.

Unfortunately, changing your foreign currency to colones could turn out to be your most unpleasant experience in Costa Rica. The levels of bureaucracy in Costa Rica's banks are unsurpassed. You may have to wait in line for more than an hour while somebody in front of you cashes in sheet upon sheet of winning lottery tickets, or has his loan payments calculated on antiquated adding machines and then transferred to record sheets by a teller with hunt-and-peck typing skills (and how they insist on using typewriters!).

And after waiting, you still may not get your money changed. After two hours in line at a provincial bank, I once had my travelers checks refused because I had no permanent address in Costa Rica. I was turned down at other banks because Visa travelers checks were out of favor (they wouldn't say why). Some visitors are refused because they have no passports, although none is required to enter the country.

Unfortunately, there are few alternatives to the banks and their sadistic methods. Severe currency controls are now in effect, and visitors may change their money only at banks and at certain hotels. Enforcement is strict, and there is no evident black market.

With a few precautions, however, you can avoid problems. Some suggestions:

Buy colones before you enter the country. Costa Rican currency is available at exchange dealers in the Los Angeles and Miami airports, often at rates more favorable than in Costa Rica itself.

Exchange a substantial amount on arriving at the airport in San José. The airport bank is relatively hassle-free.

180

Change money at your hotel, if it performs this service. The rate, however, will be slightly less favorable than at the banks.

If you must exchange money at a bank, get there early in the day, and get as much cash as you feel comfortable carrying. Normal banking hours are from 9 a.m. to 3 p.m.

Use credit cards when possible (see below).

Carry a passport for identification.

Take U. S. dollars in cash or travelers checks. Other currencies, such as Canadian dollars and sterling, are difficult if not impossible to exchange.

Only $50 in U. S. funds may be repurchased at the airport bank before leaving Costa Rica. Avoid leaving the country with extra Costa Rican money, which will be exchanged abroad at an unfavorable rate or not at all.

Credit cards—Visa, Master Card and American Express—are widely accepted in Costa Rica. You may reasonably expect to use your credit card at any hotel that charges $35 or more for a double room, and at restaurants where a meal costs $5 or more per person. The bank rate of exchange in effect on the date of your purchase will be applied (the card issuer may charge a commission as well). Be aware that some establishments will not accept credit cards at night or on weekends when their validity may not be confirmable. Be prepared to pay cash.

Money from home may be received by telegraphic or Telex transfer through a bank in San José. Make sure you know through which bank it will be sent—several have similar names. If you're not in a hurry, have an international money order sent to you by registered mail. It costs less. Regular money orders and personal checks are nearly impossible to cash.

National Parks

Costa Rica is one of the leaders in Latin America in preserving its natural treasures. More than eight percent of the country's land area has been set aside in national parks, national monuments, nature reserves, biological reserves, and recreation areas. Park planners have attempted to protect a sample of each climate and ecosystem in the country. While some parks are in remote locations, visitors are encouraged to enjoy all of them. Camping facilities, nature trails, visitors' centers and shelters are provided in most.

181

The creation of the national parks is part of a double-edged policy regarding the natural environment. Timber operations and land-clearing for farming, with the encouragement of the government, are proceeding apace, and destroying native flora and fauna at a frightening rate. A number of parks were last-minute creations that rescued unique areas from farming or tourist development just in the nick of time. But these wild areas of reduced size, even when protected, may not be able to support viable populations of endangered plant and animal species.

In most of Costa Rica's national parks, visitors will be on their own, with minimal guidance from administrators or interference from other tourists. You'll be freer than in most similar reserves to wander about at your own pace, observe wildlife, and discern the finer features of plants and geological formations. But you'll also have a greater responsibility than elsewhere both to watch out for your own safety and to tread lightly.

Visits to the national parks, except the most frequented ones (Poás, Irazú, Cahuita, Guayabo and Santa Rosa), should be preceded by inquiries at park headquarters in San José as to seasonal conditions and the current state of facilities. See the San José section of this book for the address. Park headquarters will sell you a good pamphlet guide to the parks and reserves, with information on how to get to them. A more detailed description of the parks and their wildlife, with excellent color photos (and an imperfectly rendered English text) is Mario Boza, et. al., *The National Parks of Costa Rica* (Madrid: INCAFO, 1981), available at San José bookstores.

Most of the parks are described in the text of this book. See "national parks" in the index. Parks and reserves not otherwise mentioned are:

Carrara Biological Reserve: A tropical forest area in the central Pacific coastal region.

Hitoy Cerere Biological Reserve: Rain forest on the Atlantic slope of the Talamanca mountains.

Santa Ana Recreation Area: Future home of the National Zoo, west of San José.

Post Office

Approximate postal rates are as follows: For light letters, up to 10 grams, via air mail, to the United States and Canada, 16 colones(25 cents); to Europe, 18 colones (28 cents). Post cards by air to the United States and Canada, 8 colones (12 cents); to Europe, 10 colones (16 cents).

Letters may be received in Costa Rica by having them sent to your name care of *lista de correos* (general delivery), Correo Central, San José (or any other city where you may be). There is a small charge for each letter picked up. Tell your correspondents to write neatly. Illegible foreign handwriting is responsible for many a letter going astray.

You may also receive parcels at lista de correos, but, except for books, there isn't much point in having anything sent. The customs duty usually exceeds the value of the merchandise. Tell the folks at home to send a money order instead.

Retirement

Many retired foreigners make their homes in Costa Rica, and why not? Comfortable houses are available for much less than in many other countries. The climate in most areas is agreeable all year. Health care is of good quality, and most people are friendly. The cost of living is moderate, and household help is affordable.

Another attraction is the liberal law that grants special status to retired foreigners with monthly incomes of $600 per month. Such persons may become residents with all the rights of Costa Ricans except working and voting. They pay no tax on foreign income, may import a car free of duty, and are granted a generous customs-duty exemption for household goods.

Not all retirees find Costa Rica to their liking, however. Some find it difficult to communicate in Spanish. Trips back home are expensive. Suitable housing is lacking outside of the Central Valley and a few coastal developments. Many goods carry high prices, especially foreign liquor and appliances. Currency fluctuations and inflation make it difficult to predict future living costs. In some cases, the good life can get to be boring.

For most retirees, the advantages outweigh the disadvantages. Assistance in obtaining retired-residence status is given by the Costa Rican Tourist Board (see "More Information," below).

Shopping

Few traditional handicrafts—articles made on a small scale for home use—survive in Costa Rica. Items in this category are pottery, handwoven textiles, and some woodware. Non-traditional handicraft and souvenir items available in San José are leather-work, hardwood carvings, reproductions of pre-Columbian arti-facts, and the usual run of straw hats, t-shirts, ashtrays and the like. You should have no trouble finding these, but just in case, I've given the names and locations of some stores in the shopping section of the San José chapter of this book. Outside of the capital, handicrafts may be found at outlets of ANDA, the gov-ernment-sponsored handicraft organization.

Don't overlook some of the non-souvenir items that are much cheaper in Costa Rica than at home. Stop into a supermarket and pick up a pound or two or three of coffee. Most brands are ground and come in a cellophane pack, which is poor at retain-ing flavor. Volio coffee, however, is also sold in whole-bean form for grinding at home. Tropical delicacies such as palmito (heart of palm) are priced reasonably. Hot pepper sauces, chocolates, tropical fruit preserves and much else could fill up those empty spaces in your luggage.

Once you start in at the supermarket, take a look at some general department stores (almacenes) and shopping centers (centros comerciales). You may or may not find goods you like at prices to suit your budget, but you'll get an idea of what the Costa Ricans buy and what they have to pay.

Student and Youth Travel

OTEC, the Costa Rican Organization for Youth and Student Travel, offers travel services, domestic airline discounts, low-cost accommodations in San José, and discounts in museums, stores and national parks to holders of the International Student Iden-tity Card. Student visitors may obtain details at OTEC's central offices, Avenida 3, Calles 3/5, San José, tel. 220866.

Taxes

Almost all goods and services in Costa Rica are subject to a 10 percent value-added tax ("i.v.a."). Hotel rooms are subject to an additional 3 percent tourism tax. At the airport, the exit tax is approximately eight dollars.

Telegrams

International telegrams are handled by Radiográfica Costarricense, Calle 1, Avenida 5, San José. Telegrams may be dictated by dialing 123, or by transmitting them through your hotel operator. In all cases, the rates are quite high—usually 50 cents per word or more.

Telephones

Costa Rica has a modern, direct-dial telephone system, with more lines per inhabitant than almost any other nation in Latin America. Phones in Costa Rica may be reached from the United States by dialing 011-506 followed by the six digits of the Costa Rican telephone number. From Costa Rica, numbers in other countries may be reached by dialing the international access code (011 for the United States or Canada) followed by the area code and number, or through hotel operators. Calls to most parts of the States cost about $2 per minute; to Canada, $3 per minute; to Europe, $6 per minute. If calling from a hotel, ascertain first any additional charges, or else call collect.

Within Costa Rica, there are no area codes. Any number can be reached simply by dialing its six digits. Dial local numbers carefully to avoid erroneous long-distance charges! In a few remote locations, your call will reach a local operator, who will connect you with your party. Long-distance calls within Costa Rica may be placed through your hotel or a pay phone (if you can find one that works). Rates are moderate. From San José to Liberia, for example, a three-minute call from a public phone will cost about 25 cents. From a private phone, the charge is about 70 cents. You'll pay more if you call through your hotel operator.

The service numbers for telephone number information, etc., given in the San José section, are valid throughout the country.

Time

Costa Rica is on Central Standard Time, equivalent to Greenwich Mean Time less six hours.

Tipping

A ten-percent service charge is added, by law, to all restaurant bills, so there's no need to leave any additional amount unless service is especially good.

At hotels, give the porter 25 to 50 cents (15 to 30 colones) per bag for carrying your luggage. Chambermaids will appreciate your leaving the equivalent of a dollar or two if you've stayed for a few days.

Taxi drivers are never tipped, nor are tour guides, except for special kindnesses.

When in doubt about whether or how much to tip, remember that a tip is a reward for good service. Poor service means no tip.

Weights and Measures

Costa Rica is firmly on the metric system. Gasoline, juice and milk are sold by the liter, fabrics by the meter, tomatoes by the kilọ. Gone are the days when visitors were confused by a hodge-podge of yards, varas, manzanas, fanegas, caballerias, gallons, and assorted other English and old Spanish measures.

Old usages survive mainly in giving directions. People will usually say 100 *metros* (meters) to indicate a city block, but you'll sometimes hear 100 *varas*. In fact, a block is closer to 100 varas, a vara being an old Spanish yard, equivalent to 33 inches or .835 meters.

What to Take and Wear

When packing for your visit to Costa Rica, keep in mind that the climate is moderate. For San José and the Central Valley, take what you would wear during the spring at home. A light sweater or jacket may be required for the evening, especially during the dry season. For early-morning excursions to the frosty heights of volcanoes, you'll do best to dress in layers, perhaps a sweater over a shirt and t-shirt, with layers coming off as the temperature climbs.

For visits to either coast, you'll want lightweight clothing, preferably all-cotton. Essential items will be a bathing suit, a few shirts or blouses, shorts, and a pair of sandals. Take one long-sleeved top and slacks in case you overexpose yourself to sun. The sultry coasts also require sunglasses, and a hat to keep the sun off your head. Cheap straw hats are widely available in Costa Rica, but the fit is often tight on gringos.

In the rainy months, from April to December, and for trips to the Caribbean, you may want to take a folding umbrella or a light raincoat, though neither is essential if you won't be straying far from your hotel or tour bus.

If you'll be traveling by bus and train, a travel alarm will come in handy for early departures. Hotel wake-up calls are unreliable.

In general, informal clothing is suitable. Even in the large cities, you may dine at your hotel in slacks and sport shirt or blouse. At the best restaurants, however, and at formal events, such as concerts at the national theater, a dress or jacket and tie are appropriate. Costa Ricans value a neat appearance (just look at how they dress!) and regard visitors who wear patched clothing with puzzlement. Shorts are not worn in San José.

Campers, and those staying at budget hotels in the lowlands, will want to take insect repellent. Good, comfortable shoes are necessary if you plan to do any walking. Tennis or jogging shoes will do.

Bring a moderate amount of reading material if your visit will center on San José, where English-language books are available, or a pile of books for a beach holiday. Film is expensive, so bring more than you think you'll need. Bring your own cigars or pipe tobacco. Pick up a few duty-free bottles of liquor on the way down if you have a favorite brand. Take sufficient deodorant, shave cream, etc. Sportsmen will want to take all the equipment they anticipate needing for fishing or camping.

In general, remember that anything imported or mechanical is likely to be much more expensive in Costa Rica than at home. So if your tape recorder or radio or some other gadget is indispensable to your being, take it along.

More Information

Costa Rica's Tourist Board (Instituto Costarricense de Turismo) is one of the more cooperative and helpful organizations of its type. Conveniently for U.S. residents, it has a toll-free number, 800-327-7033 (in Florida, 305-358-2150). For information by mail, write to 200 S. E. First Street, Suite 400, Miami, FL 33131; or to the branch office at 3540 Wilshire Blvd., no. 404, Los Angeles, CA 90010 (tel. 800-762-5909, or 800-762-5900 in California); or to the main office at Apartado Postal 777, San José, Costa Rica (tel. 231733).

Items available from the tourist board are a map of Costa Rica, a list of hotels in the moderate and higher-priced ranges, a general information folder, and brochures for individual hotels.

For detailed topographical maps, write to the Instituto Geográfico Nacional at the address given under "Maps" in the San José chapter.

For fishing information, call or write the offices of the fishing camps mentioned in coverage of the Caribbean coastal areas in this book.

Travel agents who are familiar with Costa Rica are a good source of information. If yours is not, try Americas Tours and Travel, 1218 Third Ave., Seattle, WA 98101, tel. 800-553-2513.

Useful books about Costa Rica include:

John and Mavis Biesanz, *Costa Rican Life.* New York: Greenwood, reprinted 1979.

Richard Biesanz, et. al., *The Costa Ricans.* Englewood Cliffs: Prentice-Hall, 1982.

(Both of the above books cover many aspects of Costa Rican society. The first, originally published in 1945, is regarded by many as a classic.)

Beatrice Blake and Anne Becher, *The New Key to Costa Rica.* An affectionate guide, recently updated, especially useful for its coverage of San José and information relative to long-term stays.

Ellen Searby, *The Costa Rican Traveller.* Juneau: Windham Bay Press, 1985. A guide with numerous photos, and detailed coverage of hotel facilities.

Mario Boza, et. al., *The National Parks of Costa Rica.* Madrid: Incafo, 1981. As mentioned before, the translation is shaky, but the color photos and information on flora and fauna are solid.

Hilary Bradt, *Backpacking in Mexico and Central America.* Boston: Bradt Enterprises, 1983. Includes descriptions of hikes in Costa Rica's national parks.

Most of the above titles are available in San José bookstores.

Index

190

191

192

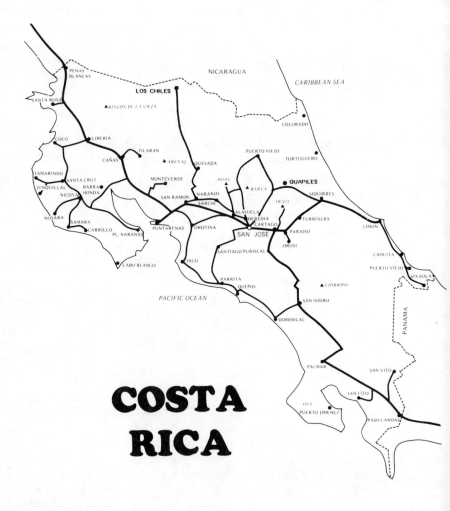

COSTA RICA

Approximate scale:

100 kilometers

Map for orientation only